BATTLES FOUGHT ON IRISH SOIL

BATTLES FOUGHT ON IRISH SOIL

A COMPLETE ACCOUNT

SEAN MCMAHON

LONDUBH BOOKS

First published in 2010 by

Londubh Books

18 Casimir Avenue, Harold's Cross, Dublin 6w, Ireland

www.londubh.ie

1 3 5 4 2

Cover by redrattledesign.com; cover image courtesy of the Natioanl Library of Ireland

Origination by Londubh Books; map of battle sites by David Parfrey

Printed in Ireland by ColourBooks, Baldoyle Industrial Estate, Dublin 13

ISBN: 978-1-907535-03-1

Contents

INTRODUCTION

When Wordsworth wrote 'The Solitary Reaper' in 1805, a poem that included the line: 'For old unhappy far-off things and battles long ago', he felt he was on safe ground. Battles were thankfully a thing of the past. The last battle on English soil had been at Sedgemoor in 1685, when Monmouth tried unsuccessfully to topple the Jacobite James II. Culloden, the last Scots battle – the one about which the solitary reaper sang – which put paid to the dream of kingship of James II's Jacobite grandson, had taken place in 1746, fifty-nine years earlier. Ireland, if Wordsworth thought about it at all, was a rather unfortunate but docile part of Greater Britain. In an age of peace, wars and their battles happened somewhere else and were the concern merely of the standing army.

Even before the coming of the Vikings, Ireland was not noted for its peacefulness. The great power blocks of the Cenél nEogáin and the Cenél Conaill – the first centred in Tyrone, the second in Donegal – regularly fought each other over territory and succession and had occasion to put manners on internal clans who were getting above themselves. It was this readiness among the Irish to resort to conflict that caused Chesterton to write:

For the great Gaels of Ireland
Are the men that God made mad,
For all their wars are merry,
And all their songs are sad.

Since Ireland is an island, most of its wars have been in reaction to invasion (including one of the battles of Moytura) and nearly all were unsuccessful. Most of the recognisable battles delineated here were against Norsemen, Normans and the offspring of these marauders, the perennial and rooted intruders, the British. The last copybook affair in Ireland was Aughrim in 1691, the affrays since that date an unfortunate feature of recurring attempts at insurrection in the distressful country.

For the purposes of this book, to the series of formal battles associated with this struggle of more than a millennium with the neighbouring realm have been added older and unhappier fields and newer but just as bloody encounters, extending the list to include the affrays of the nineteenth and the insurrections of the twentieth centuries. The Easter Rising of 1916, the Tan War and the terrible civil conflict that followed had their share of confrontations that involved armies, tactics, plans of attack – and casualties – so they are included.

Less bloody homeland affairs like the Battle of the Diamond in 1795 that saw the foundation of the Orange Order and the Battle of the Bogside in 1969 that brought the British army on to the streets of Derry, where they stayed for nearly forty years, were too important in their consequences to exclude. And because the dreamtime stories of the two battles of Moytura and the events featured in the *Táin Bó Cuailgne* helped to form the Irish psyche, they too feature in the martial array.

Although individual battles are described in this book, certain groups are nested as part of wider conflicts, such as the Nine Years' War (1594-1603) and the Rebellion of 1798. In spite of this the book is designed to be picked up and opened at will, every battle standing on its own, without reference to other engagements.

Sean McMahon, Derry, January 2010

The Two Battles of Moytura

Mythology has universally been a source of explanation among unlettered but non-primitive peoples for such mysteries as life, death and the seasons' change, artfully mixed with persistent folk memories. It is the attempt by aboriginal people at self-portrait and the preservation of age-old tradition. Irish mythology was as complete and as many-faceted as those of Greece and Rome. It had its own detailed pantheon, with gods of war, love, wisdom and the rest as in the Mediterranean tales. The earliest orally preserved belief was in a series of magical invasions, with each indigenous people falling victim to or being enslaved by successive new-comers. This may indeed describe in folk memory the reality of the country's past. As such it is as tenable a lore as Homer's *Iliad* was of real Ionian battles long ago, although it was preserved as oral lore until the scribes in the monasteries carefully recorded it centuries later, sometimes mitigating what they regarded as too blatant immorality.

Moytura, or to give it is name in Old Irish, *Mag Tuiread*, means the 'plain of the pillars', probably because of the great number of megalithic monuments to be found there. It is given as the title of two Connacht battles, the earlier one taking place on the southern part of the plain north-east of Cong on the Galway-Mayo border and the second fought twenty-seven years later near Ballinafad at Lough Arrow in County Sligo. In each case the victors were the Tuatha Dé Danaan, in the first as foreign usurpers, subduing the native Fir Bolg, and in the second in a struggle against the grotesque and evil Fomorians. These victors are revered in later folklore as the old gods of Ireland. Their name signifies the people of the ancient mother goddess Dana and they came as the fifth wave of colonists, ready to enslave the menial Fir Bolg. These people, as their name 'Bag Men' suggests, were labourers and had none of the divine powers associated with the Tuatha Dé Danaan. The belief was that in their native Greece they were an underclass forced to carry bags of good soil to fertilise rocky areas. The date of the Dé Danaan arrival was significantly 1 May and, as if to indicate their intention to stay, they burned the 300 ships that had brought them to Connacht.

At the start of the conflict the earthy Fir Bolg were aware of nothing unusual but the presence of a pervasive mist and when the Dé Danaan finally materialised a parley was arranged between Sreng, the champion of the Fir Bolg, and Bres, the chief warrior of the newcomers. Bres demanded that the natives cede half of Ireland peacefully or give battle. Erc, the king of the Fir Bolg, who had been apprised of the coming of the strangers in a prophetic dream, chose battle. It lasted for four days with great losses on both sides. During the fighting, Nuada, the Dé Danaan king, had his right arm severed to the shoulder by Sreng.

In a further parley Erc accepted Nuada's offer that the Fir Bolg should retain one of the four provinces. The choice of Connacht was followed by an accepted peace but since Nuada was now physically imperfect he could no longer be king and Bres ruled the three assigned provinces for seven years. He was deposed then because of his cruel treatment of his fellow Dé Danaan. Meanwhile Nuada had recourse to the Dian Cecht, the god of medicine, who made him a silver hand, so that he was named for posterity as Airgetlám ('Silver Hand'). Dian's cleverer son, Miach, later made him a real hand by causing flesh to grow over his father's silver device. By this means Nuada was later restored to the kingship but his nickname persisted.

The second battle was fought against the evil Fomorians, urged on by Bres, who, it was discovered, had Fomorian blood. These grotesque people originated in Tory Island and had as king Balor of the Evil Eye, the Irish Cyclops. They represented the forces of wickedness in Irish mythology and were usually depicted as having single arms and legs as well as eyes. In the second battle their forces were led by Bres and they had as their special weapon the eye of Balor that brought death to all who looked upon it. The Dé Danaan army was led by Lugh, the sun-god, grandson of Balor, much against the giant's will. During the fighting Balor killed Nuada but was himself killed when Lugh's sling shot knocked his eye out through the back of his head, killing many of the Fomorians who were unlucky enough to gaze upon it. The battle continued until the Fomorians were driven into the sea, as their name suggests (Fo means under and muir means sea). The traitor Bres survived the carnage and was spared on the condition that he teach the Tuath Dé Danaan the arts of ploughing, sowing and reaping.

The accounts of the battles indicate that spear, sword and shield were already the weapons used and single combat a persistent feature. In Christian times the bookish monks wrote down the oral sagas and derogated the Tuatha Dé Danaan to the level of heroes, denying them deity since there was but one true God. In later folklore they became *Na Daoine Beaga*, the Little People, whose possible malevolence had judiciously to be countered.

THE BATTLE AT THE FORD

Cúchulainn, the Irish Achilles, plays a significant part in several of the mythological sagas but most notably in the *Táin Bó Cúailgne* ('The Cattle-Spoil of Cooley'). He was certainly a demigod and his supreme moment was in the single combat with his friend and foster-brother, Ferdiad.

Cúchulainn's given name was Setanta and from childhood he demonstrated the preternatural gifts inherited from his true father, the sun-god Lugh. He had the physical ability to race and catch again a ball that he had hit with his camán. Once as a youth he had been attacked by a guard dog of Culann, the magic smith, and killed it; in recompense he offered to act in its place as Culann's hound, hence his adult name. He and Ferdiad had been taught the martial arts by their Amazonian Scottish tutor, Scáthach, on the Isle of Skye, and were intended to be brothers-in-arms. Cúchulainn's capacity as a warrior was enhanced by his sword Cailidcheann ('hard-headed'), by the battle spasm, which contorted his body, and the *Gae Bolg*, a kind of umbrella spear with thirty barbs that had one entry point but opened up inside the body, causing mortal wounds. Scáthach had taught him how to launch it with his foot. The battle spasm or frenzy, used only *in extremis*, was terrifying to look at and hard to recover from. It took immersion in three tubs of ice-cold water used serially to bring this about and once when the douche failed a parade of naked women, led out from Emain Macha, the headquarters of King Conchobar's Red Branch Knights, by Mugháin, the king's wife, was required.

The Battle at the Ford was the last action in the war between Connacht and Ulster over Donn Cuailgne, the brown bull of Cooley, in County Louth, near to where Cúchulainn fought the waves. Medb, queen of Connacht, wanted to add Donn to her herd but, having failed to acquire it by financial and sexual persuasion, declared war on Ulster, of which Louth was then part. The Ulster warriors had fallen under the curse of the dying Macha, whose husband, Cruinnic MacAgnomain, boasted that she could out race the fastest of the King of Ulster's horses. When she refused on the grounds of being pregnant, the King threatened her with death . She won the race but died, but not before she cursed the men of Ulster to suffer the pangs of childbirth for five days and four nights at the time of Ulster's greatest difficulty. Cúchulainn, one of the few exempt from the curse, was forced to face Medb's army alone. He demanded his right of single combat and all Medb's warriors fell before the might of the Ulster champion. She tried all the arts of magic but they too were ineffective.

Medb's last hope was Ferdiad, who, once an adherent of Conchobar, had joined the army of Connacht because of the Ulster king's cruelty. The two heroes seemed equally matched, both trained by Scáthach and preternaturally gifted as warriors. Ferdiad, whose epithet was Conganchness, ('with skin like horn') was unassailable by sword or spear, except in his body orifices, while Cúchulainn had the *Gae Bolg*. At first Ferdiad refused to fight him but Medb and her daughters, having offered him extreme sexual favours and been rejected, threatened to 'rhyme' him: pillory him in verse for cowardice.

The two heroes met at a ford on the little river Dee in the southern part of Cúchulainn's territory of Muirthemne, the plain of Louth between the Boyne River and Dundalk. On the first day, with heroic courtesy, Cúchulainn allowed Ferdiad choice of weapons because '…it was you was the first to reach the ford.' Ferdiad chose 'casting weapons' and so the day was spent. Next morning it was Cúchulainn's turn and he opted for their 'great broad spears'. So 'they continued to cut and to wound and to redden the other from the twilight of the early morning till the fall of evening.' The third day they used 'their great broad swords'. The day-long battles were slowly weakening even these champions.

The fight lasted the traditional four days, leaving both demigods exhausted but still vertical, with Ferdiad seeming to be stronger. On the morning of the fourth day, weak with loss of blood, Cúchulainn called for his charioteer Laeg to fetch him the Gae Bolg. Laeg floated it down the river and Cúchulainn trapped it with his foot. He aimed a spear at Ferdiad's face, and Ferdiad instinctively lifted his shield to deflect it. With his anus exposed he could not prevent the terrible thirty-barbed spear thrown accurately by Cúchulainn's right foot from entering his body and opening inside his abdomen. When he saw that his old comrade was dead Cúchulainn grieved as for a brother, groaning, 'O Ferdiad, you were betrayed to your death; your last end was sorrowful; you to die, I to be living; our parting for ever is a grief for ever.'

Cúchulainn did not long survive Ferdiad. Weak with loss of blood and lack of food he had himself bound to a pillar. He might even then have survived but that Mórrígán, the goddess of war, death and slaughter, whose sexual advances he had earlier rejected, perched on his shoulder in her favourite shape of the raven to show that he was dying. The iconic figure of the warrior dying at his pillar while the bird perched on his shoulder, sculpted by Oliver Sheppard (1865-1941) in 1912, is now in the GPO in Dublin. The Battle of the Ford is recalled in Ardee (*Baile Átha Fhirdhia*), the name in modern Irish of the town in County Louth where the mythical confrontation took place.

Cul Dremne, 561 AD

The battle of Cul Dremne belongs to that era of Irish history where myth and fact fit snugly with the lives of saints. The battle was fought on the plain where the prow of the upended vessel that is Ben Bulben points towards Drumcliffe Bay. Its configuration suggests it as a significant boundary between north and west, Ulster and Connacht and the Southern and the Northern Uí Néill. The outstanding figure associated with the battle, whether justly or not, is Colum Cille (*c.* 521-97), the greatest of the Irish-born saints and founder of many monasteries including Swords, Durrow and primarily Iona (in 653).

The only textual association of the saint with the battle comes from *Vita Columbae*, ('The Life of Columba'), by Adomnán (*c.* 628-704), the ninth abbot of Iona, in which he dates Colum Cille's self-imposed *bán-martra* ('white martyrdom') of exile as two years after the battle. The idea of 'white martyrdom' was a potent one. In a country free from religious persecution monks were in no danger from 'red' martyrdom, which they would willingly have suffered. 'Green' martyrdom allowed the sufferer to remain at home and sanctify himself with fasting and hard labour but *bán-martra* was to the home-loving Irish a kind of death. Leaving Ireland with its intricate familial structures made exile a true martyrdom.

Details of the action are obscure but the Ulster armies roundly defeated the rest and the leader of the southern Uí Néill, Diarmait mac Cerbaill, who had claimed the high-kingship of Tara in 544, was killed on Lough Neagh in 565. The causes of the battle are obscure; dynastic struggle was commonplace in the Ireland of the time. Diarmait's ambition was to extend the power of the position of *ard rí* and the powerful northern tribes were determined to thwart this. Adomnán had claimed Diarmait as a Christian but many historians believe the war might have been supported by the Church because of Diarmait's persistence in inappropriate pagan practices. This would have explained Colum Cille's involvement in the battle and one of many stories associated with him is that his corpse bore the marks of old wounds. His aristocratic familial connections made it almost incumbent upon him to involve himself on the side of the northern Uí Néill, perhaps as a kind of super army chaplain. Certainly the annalists give the credit for the northern victory to the saint's blessing of the troops and the continuing prayers said during the conflict.

Cul Dremne seems to have stayed in folk memory as a particularly bloody encounter since it gives the total number of the southern dead as 3000. Colum Cille's confessor in the legend imposed upon him the penance of saving as many souls for Christ as had died in the battle. This was accepted for years as the true reason for the *ban martra* that took him with twelve disciples to the nearest Inner Hebridean island from which no vestige of Ireland could be seen. The implication was that he had somehow been responsible for instigating the war against Diarmait. There were two possible motives for this: revenge for a wrong done him over a question of the death of a hostage in the saint's care and personal spleen at one of the earliest intellectual property disputes. As the story goes, Colum Cille, who was famous as a penman, had written out without the owner's permission a copy of a psalter which was the property of the great Finian (*c.* 493-579) of Movilla, near modern Newtownards in County Down. The work had been long and laborious and the result was very beautiful. When Finian claimed the copy as his property Colum Cille was deeply vexed. To avoid internal monastic recrimination the matter was referred to Diarmait for adjudication.

As *Betha Colaim Chille*, the sixteenth-century life of the saint written under the aegis of Maghnus Ó Domhnaill (d. 1563), Lord of Tír Chonaill, records, Diarmait gave the following judgement: '*Le gach boin a boinín; le gach leabhar a leabhrán.*' (To every cow its calf; to every book its version.') The saint, always appearing in the legends as a man capable of great rages, swore vengeance. When shortly afterwards Curnan, the son of the king of Connacht, who was under the protection of the saint, was executed by Diarmait for an accidental killing, Colum Cille began a campaign against the high king that ended with the defeat at Cul Dremne. The character that emerges from all this seems true to the historical short-tempered figure.

As to the literal truth of the battle and its origins, lack of knowledge makes the picture very incomplete. In fact Diarmait seems to have been the aggressor and it was his thrust north-west that alerted the Ulster leaders. He was met by an alliance of the descendants of the proto-Eogan and those of Conall Gulban, the son of the original hero-figure, the semi-mythical Niall Noígiallach ('Niall of the Nine Hostages'), who was also an ancestor of Colum Cille. In the circumstances, chroniclers, who liked coherence and symmetry in their stories, could hardly have excluded such a giant figure from their accounts of the time. The only suspicious element in all of the tales is the seamless linearity of the events described. Chroniclers tend to leave no gaps; historians have to.

THE VIKING WARS 917-1014

Confey (917) and Tara (980)

The years 795-1200 in Irish history are conveniently if not very precisely labelled as the time of the Viking terror. The word 'Viking' comes from Old English and meant 'pirate' and it was a just description of the raiders from Norway and to a lesser extent Denmark. They had no fear of death because of their belief in the warriors' paradise of Valhalla; this was a kind of Scandinavian *Tír na nÓg* in the form of a banqueting hall where dead heroes spent an eternity in joy and feasting, drinking mead and ale out of the skulls of their victims. The Scandinavians were sorely affected by poor harvests and overcrowding at home and they found Ireland a convenient place to plunder and later to colonise, raiders becoming traders.

The most famous of the battles involving the Vikings that were fought on Irish soil was Clontarf but the four centuries of their activity in Ireland are full of confrontations. As well as a just reputation for fierce fighting and skilful navigation they brought from their homelands a fine instinct for commerce and town planning. We who are so wise after the events can only regret that assimilation was so bloody and partial and took so long, and that their influence was not more pervasive. The naval defeat of the Vikings – one of the few since they were excellent sailors and had virtually iron-clad ships because of their device of hanging their shields over the sides – in Lough Foyle (*c.* 860) by Áed Findlaith, king of Aileach, set back the development of Derry by hundreds of years.

As Ireland at the time was a collection of small, usually

warring, states called *tuatha*, each with its own king, the national response to the *Lochlannaigh*, as they were initially called, was sporadic, weak and incohesive. As the centuries passed the now native Danes and Norwegians found themselves in alliances with Irish power groups, especially in the east and south of the country. The tenth century saw the influx of the greatest number of invaders and the best equipped but at times they were resisted with unusual ferocity by sufficient numbers of natives.

In the battle of *Cenn Fuait* in 917 a strong force of Norsemen defeated a Leinster army led by King Augaire mac Aiella and recaptured Dublin, which was essentially a Viking construct. The location is thought by some scholars to be that of Confey, near Leixlip in County Kildare. The 'heathen' were led by Sitriuc, the grandson of Ímar, almost certainly born in Dublin. (Ímar -Ivar in Norwegian – was from Norway and had ruled from 853 to 873; he was recognised as the first leader of the *Lochannaigh* in Dublin.) Later they met an army of the Irish led by Niall, 'son of Aed, king of Ireland' that had fought its way from Clonmel. The combined Irish army was unusually large and coherent, including many nobles from different tuatha in the south and east of the country.

The history of the time becomes very complicated because of the frequency of alliances with the Ostmen around Dublin. Later they confronted an army, the 'dark foreigners' at Confey and fought 'between terce and noon'. (Terce was one of the three divisions of the divine office of the Church, the equivalent of 9am.) In the three hours of the battle the fighting must have been intense, as six hundred of the Irish warriors were lost. The flat terrain meant that the fighting would have been hand-to-hand after an initial use of spears. Among the fallen, according to the 16th-century *Annals of Ulster*, were Ugaire, son of Ailill, king of Leinster, Mael Mórda, son of Muirecán, king of eastern Life, Mael Maedóc, son of Diarmait, bishop of Leinster, Ugrán, son of Cennéitig. King of Laois and other leaders and nobles. The account ends with the stark sentence: 'Sitriuc, grandson of Ímar, entered Áth Cliath.'

Sixty-three years later the Norse of Dublin were defeated by Máel Sechnaill mac Domhnaill, the new head of the southern Uí Néill in the Battle of Tara. The Dubliners called in reinforcements from the Inner Hebrides and the Isle of Man, with which they had fraternal connections. Their commander was Olaf Cuaran – or Amlaíb Cuarán, also known as Óláfr Sigtryggsson. The Irish forces were drawn mainly from the kingdom of Mide (present-day Meath) with support from both south and north, even the enigmatic and exclusivist Ulster chieftains offering help. The Irish were, in a sense, on home ground, and their victory over the Norse may even have been more complete than that of Clontarf, thirty-four years later. In fact, the Norse, did not lose Dublin. Olaf resigned from his office as unworthy for the task and is said to have spent the remainder of his life as a lay anchorite on Iona. By then, thanks to Colum Cille and his successors, the Gall (the Fionn Gall were the blonde Norwegian warriors, the Dubh Gall were largely from Denmark) had embraced Christianity.

Máel Sechnaill besieged the town closely but did not occupy it, preferring to accept the dole of valuables and slaves that were his price for withdrawing his victorious army. The effect on the Dublin Ostmen (the term they preferred) was further contraction but with the admixture of Danish commercial instincts and Norwegian courage the 'Fort of the Dane' as Louis MacNeice called it, settled down to an entrepreneurial role, called variously Hurdleford or Blackpool. By the end of the tenth century, Ostmen had also established themselves in the towns they had built at Waterford (*Vethrafjorthr*, 'the ford of Father Odin'), Wexford (*Weissfjord*), Cork and Limerick.

Glen Máma
30 December 999

The battle for which the various historical annals are the sources was fought in winter when a Leinster-Dublin army was defeated by the combined forces of Brian Boru (d. 1014), the Dalcassian king who ruled most of Munster, and Máel Sechnaill (Malachy) II, who was King of Meath and was anxious to be regarded as *ardrí Érenn*. (He was the Malachy who in Thomas Moore's song, 'Let Erin Remember', 'wore the collar of gold that he won from the proud invader'.)

Máel Sechnaill was for many years the adversary of the more ambitious Brian, who, coming from an obscure *tuath* in East Clare, had made himself the most powerful man in Ireland. They met at Clonfert near Shannonbridge, County Galway, in 997 and hammered out a working agreement. Máel Sechnaill assumed the authority to make a pact with Brian to divide the sovereignty of Ireland between them, Máel Sechnaill to be the titular head of the northern half, the *Leth Cuinn* ('Conn's half') while Brian accepted the lordship of the southern half, the *Leth Moga* ('Mug Nuadat's half'), concepts dating from prehistory.

This uneasy truce was frequently broken, with many attacks by Brian, until, in 1002, Máel Sechnaill submitted, acting thereafter as Brian's ally, except, crucially, at Clontarf when he held off his armies until the battle was won and Brian dead. The native Leinstermen, constantly at enmity with the rest of the country, found it convenient to make alliance with the Ostmen around Dublin, a compact that suited the Ostmen equally well. It was the belligerent revolt of the Leinstermen against Brian that made the battle necessary. According to the *Annals of the Four Masters* (1632-6) the battle was the subject of a prophecy of doom for the Norse-Leinster alliance:

> *From the victorious overthrow they shall retreat*
> *Till they reach past the wood northwards,*
> *And Áth-Cliath the fair shall be burned*
> *After ravaging the Leinster plain*

Originating in Dublin, the two armies met in a narrow valley called Glen Máma, a place of extreme iconic significance to Leinster kings, near the modern town of Dunlavin in County Wicklow. Brian had expected that the Leinster armies would try to reach Dunlavin, where the mountains meet the plain, so he was able to cut off their retreat . They rallied again at Lemmonstown in Wicklow and in a battle that was described in the (twelfth-century) *Cogadh Gaedhal re Gallaibh*, ('War of the Irish against the Foreigners') the propaganda compilation commissioned by Brian's great-grandson, as 'bloody, furious, red, valiant and heroic, rough, cruel and heartless' the 'Danish' army was vanquished. There was no let-up; a band of cavalry that tried to ford the Liffey at Ballymore Eustace was allowed to perish in the morass at nearby Tubber.

Those combatants who were able to retreat headed north to Hollywood but these too were pursued by Brian and it was his son Murchadh who discovered Máel Mórda, the Leinster king, sheltering in the branches of a tree. He was later ransomed by his sister Gormflaith and led the Leinstermen at Clontarf. As a result of the battle of Glen Máma, seven thousand of the Norsemen (the *Gaill* of the Ua Briain compilation) were killed in that borderland of Wicklow and Kildare. That figure is all the more significant when one considers that most armies at the time consisted of not more than two hundred men.

The victory of the coalition of Brian Boru and Máel Sechnaill, King of Meath, stilled Norse activity for at least a decade but the mutual animosity of the native Irish sharpened, and even though they and their Scandinavian allies were defeated again at Clontarf fifteen years later, the 'otherness' of the Leinstermen was to cause untold damage to Ireland for many centuries.

CLONTARF
23 APRIL 1014

Possibly the most famous battle in Irish history except for the Boyne more than five centuries later years later, Clontarf was also the one most simplified for patriot ears by the romantic historians of the nineteenth century. Any Irish schoolchild of the first half of the twentieth could give all the sad and glorious details of King Brian Boru's death in his seventy-third year by the evil and sneaky Viking mercenary Brodar just at the moment when his victorious army had effectively routed the enemy Danes and saved the country for Christendom – and on Good Friday too! The walls of village halls and primary school classrooms were often decorated with the scene in the tent: the grey-bearded saint was shown kneeling barefoot before an empty table with a plain crucifix upon it. Behind him in blue jerkin stands the wicked Brodar with horned helmet and fierce moustaches, ready to hack off the venerable head with his battleaxe. By an evil chance the king's tent lay virtually unguarded in the path of the runaway Manx Danes and, coward as he is always regarded, Brodar could not resist the ultimate prize of the king's head.

Life, Irish history and the Vikings are a great deal more complicated than that. For a start the Ostmen, as they preferred to call themselves, were almost entirely Norse, the Danes tending to colonise England and the Swedes looking to the east. The battle was not about Christianity; by the beginning of the eleventh century many of the Ostmen had accepted Christianity, mainly through intermarriage. It was about power and sovereignty and the Leinster men's instinctive rejection of a united Ireland in which they would not have hegemony. The inherent complications are made manifest when one considers that the Ostmen opposing Brian's Munster men were led by Sitric, who was Brian's son-in-law, and that Gormflaith his mother, the sister of Máel Mórda, the Leinster king who had survived the Battle of Glen Máma fifteen years earlier, had been married both to Brian and his ally, Máel Sechnaill II, King of Meath, who for some unexplained reason did not take part in the battle.

The Ostmen element of Máel Mórda's army included warriors from the Isle of Man, the Hebrides, the Orkneys and Iceland, under the supreme command of Sigurd, Lord of Orkney, who, the gossip had it, had come because the bewitching Gormflaith had offered her body as an extra inducement. Brian's forces were mainly Irish but he had a considerable number of Limerick Norse and even some mercenaries from Man who guarded the wing nearest Dublin Bay. Because there were so many Norse involved (and so many fatalities) the battle was significant enough to figure in the thirteenth-century Icelandic saga *Burnt Njal* in which Gromflaith is called Kormlada. The Irish version of the story was given in the twelfth-century *Cogadh Gaedhel re Gallaibh*, essentially a propaganda document commissioned by Brian's great-grandson and used in his claim for high-kingship against the northern Uí Néill. During the time of Clontarf, Ulster had remained aloof, enigmatic and very wet.

The battle was fought in Drumcondra, north and east of the River Tolka and close to the bay. It must have resembled two mighty fists with tightly closed fingers in bloody collision. The Leinster men had come from Tara to join the Norse as they marched out from their well-defended Dublin town. The other Norse forces had anchored their very manoeuvrable longships on the foreshore at the North Strand. The battle arrays would have been similar in composition, vanguard, battle group and relief forces placed behind; there would also have been wings ready on each side to close a circle if it was necessary. The combatants used swords and round shields, that could also be used as weapons, and javelins attached by leather thongs to the wrist of the thrower for handy retrieval. The Norse weapon of choice was the battle-axe, which needed two hands but which could be wielded with deadly effect. Sigurd was killed early on and Brodar was chased off the field by Wolf the Quarrelsome, a noted Norse warrior, (This colourfully named warrior met Brodar again and hacked him to pieces before the end of the battle.)

At seven thousand the army of Brian Boru was slightly greater in number than the Leinster alliance. Even by a crude reckoning at least ten thousand men were killed that day, with most of the Leinster-Ostmen alliance wiped out. Although Brian's army won the battle, the fact confirmed by the streams of Vikings trying to reach the safety of their ships, it was essentially a Pyrrhic victory. Among the four thousand Munster dead were Murchad, Brian's son, and *his* fifteen-year-old son Tordhbelbach, the two main hopes of continuity of Brian's plan for an Ireland ruled by one family and ultimately, perhaps, free of internal dissension. In a sense the only winner was Sitric, who observed the fighting with his mother Gormflaith from the comparative safety of the Norse town of Dublin that remained unscathed. Sitric continued to rule there until his death in 1042. Brian's hope of a sovereign nation, implied in his decision to accept the title of *Imperator Scottorum* ('Emperor of the Gael'), which was proposed by his confessor, Mael Suthain and recorded in the book of Armag, dating from 808, perished with him and Murchad. There had been a decade of peace, prosperity and aesthetic achievement in the territories ruled by Brian but now like Camelot it seemed a fleeting wisp of glory.

The Norman and Old English Era
1171-1580

DUBLIN
SEPTEMBER 1171

The disparate and disunited reaction of the Irish to the intrusion of the Vikings showed how far from being a united country the collection of warring statelets was. The only unifying system was the Church but it too was in serious need of reform. A leader with the charisma and ambition of Brian Boru was able to unite for a short while at least the south of the country but after Clontarf there was no one. The middle of the twelfth century was similar to the middle of the tenth, with Leinster as ever the ambitious troublemaker. Its king, Diarmit Mac Murchada (Dermot MacMurrough) (d. 1171), had ruled from 1132 to 1166, when he was deposed by Ruaidrí Ua Conchobair (Rory O'Connor) (d. 1198) the *ard rí* from Connacht (in fact Ireland's last *ard rí*.)) The danger he presented even to the weak measure of stability that existed that was the main reason for his being deposed as King of Leinster. To add to the gossip of the time, Mac Murchada had a personal enmity with Tigernán Ua Ruairc, king of Bréifne, centred round modern Cavan. He was accused of stealing the not-unwilling Derbforgaill (Dervorgilla), Ua Ruairc's wife, and of the greater insult of sending her back to her husband.

So far there was nothing unprecedented in the story. What had an effect for more than eight hundred years was Diarmit's next injudicious move, although it was perfectly logical at the time. When Diarmit's castle at Ferns was razed by Ruaidrí he escaped to Bristol with a few followers and his daughter Aoife on 1 August 1166. Eventually he visited Henry II (1133-89)who was touring his Angevin territories, and won from him the assent to re-establish himself as king of Leinster with whatever force he could find among the king's subjects. The dire decision was laconically described in the twelfth-century *Book of Leinster*: 'The English came into Ireland and Ireland was destroyed by them.' Henry's domain then stretched from 'the Cheviots to the Pyrenees' but Diarmait found the adventurers he needed among the Welsh-Norman lords, at least two of whom, Maurice Fitzstephen and Robert Fitzstephen, were the children of Nesta ap Rhys, the fertile and bounteous princess of Wales. Their leader was Richard de Clare (d. 1176), Earl of Pembroke, known as 'Strongbow', and Diarmait invited him to become his son-in-law with right of succession to Leinster.

Ireland's ecclesiastically lawless reputation then was such that the territorially ambitious Henry had managed to win from Pope Adrian IV (1100-59) (entirely coincidentally the only English pope) the much-disputed bull *Laudabiliter* that gave him the mission, should he choose to accept it, of reforming the Irish Church.

The advance guard of the Norman invaders, as we can conveniently call them, landed at the rocky tip of Bannow Bay in County Wexford on 1 May 1169. Their leader was Strongbow's most trusted lieutenant, Raymond le Gros. As the old couplet put it:

> At the creek of Baginbun
> Was Ireland lost and Ireland won.

The raiders, ruthless and heavily armed, soon overcame local resistance and essentially recovered Leinster, with Dublin as its capital, for Diarmait. The marriage of Strongbow and Aoife followed soon after. The sudden death of Diarmait two years later meant that Strongbow inherited the kingdom of Leinster.

At last the bewildered Irish, ineffectually led by the *ard rí* Ruaidrí Ua Conchobair, decided that the time had come to try to oust the new Gaill ('strangers'). The native Dubliners, the remainder Ostmen, who rose against the Normans, were soon shown to be weak and under-armed. A more serious threat came from a combined force of Irish, led by Ruaidrí, with support from Ua Ruairc of Bréifne and from Bréifne's nearest neighbour, the O'Carroll from Monaghan-Louth. Also on the scene was a force of Norsemen led by Haskulf, the king of the Dublin Norse, who had escaped from the beleaguered town and had managed to assemble an army of Irish Ostmen with fighting men from the Isle of Man and the Scottish islands. It is believed that they besieged the town first but were attacked and defeated on the foreshore of Dublin Bay, between the River Poddle and the Dodder. It was an oddly appropriate confrontation; the Ostmen and the Anglo-Normans were of the same blood, since both sprang from Scandinavian roots. Tough fighters as the Ostmen were, they were no match for the heavily armoured military machine that was the Norman cavalry.

Richard de Cogan was sent out to face the Ostmen on the flat littoral where Trinity College now stands. His thirty knights were greatly outnumbered but the men on steeds clad in chain mail were virtually invulnerable. It was then that Miles de Cogan, Richard's elder brother, crashed out over the Poddle to attack Haskulf's rear, cutting him off from his beached ships. While de Cogan's knights formed an impenetrable wall, his deadly archers scarcely had to take aim, so tightly packed were Haskulf's troops. With nothing but their traditional round shields and horned helmets as protection, the Ostmen were no match for their cousins, superior in equipment and tactics.

This phase of the battle went to the Normans but there was still the *ard rí* and his Irish allies to face. As well as the allies listed above, Ruaidrí had help from O'Melaghlin of Meath and Mac Duinn Sléibhe, king of Ulidia, today's Down and Antrim. They had sufficient numbers to blockade the small town of Dublin. The chroniclers of the time estimated that Ruaidrí had at his disposal in excess of 30,000 troops. He and his native Connacht followers and most of his allies made their camp at present-day Castleknock. Mac Duinn Sléibhe's army were at Clontarf and a number of faithful Leinster tribes on the opposite side of the bay at Dalkey.

As usual the Irish had no equipment with which to attempt to take the town but they could blockade it. Lorcán Ua Tuathail, known in hagiography as St Laurence O'Toole (d. 1180), one of Ireland's few canonised saints, was involved in negotiations between Strongbow and Ruaidrí, seeming to have *laissez-passer* in and out of Dublin as archbishop. The *ard rí* asked too much, requiring the Normans to retain only Dublin, Waterford and Wexford and the besieged Normans refused to be bottled up in small towns. Maurice Fitzgerald, one of the original band of Welsh adventurers, urged an attack, reminding his comrades of their uniquely isolated position: 'We are Englishmen to the Irish and Irishmen to the English', as later reported.

The main attack was against the hosting at Castleknock early on a sunny September afternoon. Raymond le Gros led with twenty knights, the twelfth-century equivalent of the Tiger tank. Next came Miles de Cogan with thirty knights, followed by the main 'battle' of forty knights led by Fitzgerald and Strongbow. The Liffey's only bridge then was just outside the west gate of the fortifications of Dublin but once the Normans were across there was little to hinder them as they charged down the Tolka valley, taking the unprepared Irish by surprise, Ruaidrí surprised in his bath. There was great slaughter then and by evening the Irish were completely routed. The victorious Normans, laden with food and arms, returned to their town.

It was Strongbow's very success that alarmed Henry II and the king's arrival in Ireland in 1171 that began England's dire involvement in Irish affairs.

Dysert O'Dea
10 May 1318

Dysert O'Dea (*Diseart Uí Dheá*='O'Dea's hermitage') is five miles south of Corofin, County Clare, and the battle fought there was a kind of sideshow during Edward Bruce's invasion of Ireland. (See the Battle of Faughart on page 46). The defeat of Richard de Clare by the combined forces of Murtagh O'Brien and his vassal Conor O'Dea spelled the end of Anglo-Norman superiority in Thomond (*Tuadh-Mhumhain* ='the northern part of Munster'). It was in O'Brien territory and, although granted by Edward I (1239-1307) to Thomas de Clare, was still effectively in the hands of the O'Briens. The de Clares used what means they could to drive a wedge between the already warring inter-tribal factions. In this the clan unwittingly cooperated. Lacking the Norman system of primogeniture, the succession structure of Irish families was inherently unstable. The system of succession was by nomination and not by right of eldest son.

By the end of the thirteenth century the factions in Thomond were led by Turlough O'Brien and his kinsman Brian O'Brien. In their struggle for kingship, each sought alliances outside the clan from whatever source: in time, Dermot, Brian's son, found an alliance with the de Clares and Donough, the grandson of Turlough, with the de Burghs of Connacht. It is difficult for us to understand the complexity of the ever-changing alliances and to comprehend the chaotic state of Ireland as a whole in this period. Thomond, being a fertile part of the country, did not suffer quite so much from the famine that afflicted the rest of the country at the time but scarcity and plague also contributed to unrest there.

By 1317 the factional O'Briens had inherited the old dissensions and instincts to settle their territorial demands by war. The old Turlough faction was now led by Murtagh and his adversary from Brian's family was yet another Donough. They met in battle at Lough Baska near the Cistercian abbey of Corcomroe in the Burren in August of that year and Murtagh's faction had an overwhelming victory.

It seemed to Richard de Clare that the time was ripe for establishing the long delayed Anglo-Norman suzerainty in the county named after his family. Murtagh was now the undisputed O'Brien and victory over his army would establish the de Clares' dominance in perpetuity. Murtagh also wanted revenge for the defeat of his O'Briens at Corcomroe.

The initial successes of the intrusive Normans in the twelfth century was due partly to the internal dissension of the Irish and partly because of their armour, their superior armaments and their use of heavily-armoured cavalry. In the century and a half since then the Irish had learned from the invader. They still preferred mobility but thick woollen undershirts and leather armour proved quite effective against the arrows and hurled spears of the enemy. They began to use trenches and sharpened stakes, and given the right topography, especially in narrow passes, set up ambushes.

The O'Dea land was bounded by the Burren, the Atlantic Ocean and the River Fergus, that flows through Ennis. The O'Deas were liegemen of the O'Briens and happy to engage with the 'Gall'. When de Clare arrived at Ruan he mustered his forces before dividing them into three parties. The first under the command of his son, also Richard, was deployed right towards Tully. He led the direct assault due west towards the O'Dea castle, while the third company went roughly south-west towards Magowna. When Conor O'Dea became aware of de Clare's triple-pronged approach he sent for his allies, the O'Connors of Corcomroe and the O'Hehirs and MacNamaras, who were based locally.

De Clare's scouts reported that a small group of the O'Deas had assembled at a ford on the Fergus near the present-day Macken Bridge. Their attention seemed to be taken up with getting a herd of cattle cross the ford. When the main de Clare force saw them they seemed a rich and easy prey. A group of them turned to face the Anglo-Normans, hurling stones, using slingshots and throwing small javelins. They then began to retreat towards a marshy ground. De Clare led the charge into what was a clever ambush, during which he was felled by O'Dea, wielding an axe. The enraged Normans drove across the river to face a much larger O'Dea force that had been in hiding in a copse on the far side. As they fell back they met a force of O'Connors who had rallied to O'Dea's call. Now with both sides strengthened with allies the hand-to-hand fighting became intense. There was great loss of life on both sides and many wounded. As the chronicles put it: '...of either set many gentlemen and many fine warriors were destroyed.' For a while the result was in the balance, even though the Normans had lost their leader. Then Murtagh, the 'true king of Thomond', arrived over Spancel Hill from the north-east where his army had been encamped; the Irish succeeded in squeezing the 'Gall' between them and wiped them out. The few who escaped made for Bunratty only to find it ablaze and de Clare's wife and children fled to the safety of Limerick. They returned to England as soon as they could and the control of Thomond passed again to warring native tribes. The power of the Anglo-Normans was completely erased in north Munster and it remained under Gaelic control for a further three hundred years.

FAUGHART
14 OCTOBER 1318

Edward (*c.* 1275-1318), brother of the more famous Robert, was as passionate a Scots patriot as the greater Bruce. He fought at Bannockburn (24 June 1314), thereby helping Robert to become king of an independent Scotland. War with England continued intermittently and he devised a plan for a Pan-Gaelic alliance against the enemy. To this end he landed with 3000 men on the Antrim coast north of Larne on 25 May 1315 and had himself proclaimed ard rí with the support of Donal O'Neill, the Cénel nEógain king, based in Tír Eogáin, the modern counties of Derry and Tyrone. He intended, with native Welsh support, to invade Wales, recapture the Isle of Man and have Edward II (1284-1327) faced by enemies north and west.

Over the next three years Edward found it necessary to fight a series of battles with the Anglo-Norman colonists. He won his first encounter at Carrickfergus, ably supported by the Earl of Moray, and there he was proclaimed ard rí. He moved south and west, devastating Norman manors including Dunadry and Rathmore. Many of the local chiefs tried to ignore him or paid him mere face-saving homage. He drove through the narrow Moyry Pass, the Gap of the North, between Newry and Dundalk, and attacked the latter, burning it to the ground and massacring both Gaelic and Anglo-Norman inhabitants.

The account of his Irish adventure was part of a laudatory poem by John Dunbar (*c.* 1320-95), Archdeacon of Aberdeen, and a member of the court of the descendants of Robert Bruce, Robert

II and Robert III. He was born perhaps two years after Edward's death in battle. His heroic poem, *The Bruce* (1375), is probably not very reliable as history but his description of Bruce as one who never refused a fight is accurate enough.

It was the worst possible time for such an expedition since not only Ireland but all western Europe was experiencing appalling famine and plague. Many whom Edward expected to support him were either too weak or not discontented enough under Anglo-Irish rule to rally to a rather dubious call. By July he had penetrated as far south as Ardee, when he was forced to retreat when opposed by two armies, one commanded by Richard de Burgh and Felim, King of Connacht and the other by Butler of Ormonde. For once he took his knights' advice and retreated north to Coleraine, which he sacked. He was able to rely on Northern clans and established his lordship over the rest of the north-west by burning Northburgh Castle (now Greencastle) in Inishowen.

Feeling now ready to meet de Burgh and Butler, Edward marched south and defeated the two armies at Connor, near the village of Kells in mid-Antrim, otherwise famous for providing the name for the present-day diocese. Over the next while he engaged with both Gaelic and Anglo-Norman armies, usually winning because of the ferocity of his Scots gallowglasses (*gallóglaigh*=foreign warriors), supplemented by an army led by his brother Robert I. They swept through Leinster but failed to take the loyal city of Dublin, consoling themselves with the sacking of Limerick. With his army weakened by famine and disease Edward now withdrew to Ulster again, where he felt safest; Robert returned to Scotland.

Little is recorded of Edward's activities for about a year and a half. His grand plan for a united Ireland with the Normans allied to the residual Gaelic chieftains – always too ambitious – was beginning to unravel. King Edward II, at last made aware that Bruce constituted a real threat to his dominion of Ireland, and frightened that he might lose sovereignty as he had in

Scotland, finally sent a well-equipped English army under John de Bermingham, 1st Earl of Louth, to deal with the adventurer. Bruce marched south to meet him and they sighted each other at the hill of Faughart, four miles north of Dundalk. The place had long been revered as the birthplace of St Brigid and at the start of the fourteenth century it marked the northern boundary of the Pale.

There are few reliable details of the battle and Barbour's account in verse is inevitably suspect. Bruce's commanders urged him to wait for reinforcements thought to be near at hand but Bruce in his impetuosity would not brook any delay:

> *Now help quha will, for sekirly*
> *This day, but mair baid, fecht I will!*

His Irish allies informed him that they would not *fecht* (fight) and climbed the hill for a better view of the proceedings. The English archers, anticipating Agincourt by nearly a hundred years, poured a murderous hail of arrows on Bruce's men, while de Bermingham's infantry crashed through his lines of gallowglasses. The heavy cavalry charged on the flanks and Bruce's much debilitated Scots were scattered. Still he rallied them and with the help of the promised reinforcements charged the English soldiers again, sending them back down the hill. Bruce might well have pulled it off but that he himself was killed. The cause of death is disputed. One unlikely story was that a jongleur arrived on the battlefield, now won by the Scots, and while entertaining Bruce brained him with a ball and chain. A more likely account is that he was killed by a soldier called John Maupas *viriliter cum magno honore* whose own dead body was found by the English forces on top of the quondam ard rí.

KNOCKDOE
19 AUGUST 1504

Knockdoe's name in Irish, *Cnoc na dTua* ('Battle-axe Hill') is a linguistic memorial to the largest battle ever fought between native Irishmen, although most of the hard fighting was done by gallowglasses (*gallóglaigh*=foreign warriors), mercenaries from the Hebrides. Their leaders, usually clan chieftains, were rewarded with grants of land by the Irish lords who commissioned their services in hours of need. In time, by this process, the Boyles, Gallaghers, MacSweeneys, MacDonalds, MacCabes and MacLeods became part of the aristocracy of Gaelic Ireland. The first three of these were assigned nicknames that they retained because of perceived or imaginary idiosyncrasies: *Na Baoilligh Bheadaí* ('the fastidious Boyles'), *Gallachóirigh na gCipín Doite* ('the Gallaghers of the fire-tempered staves') and *Clann tSuibhne na Miodóg* ('the Sweeneys of the daggers'). By the beginning of the sixteenth century they formed a military elite used by both the Gaelic and the Anglo-Irish lords. They equipped themselves with the latest in military equipment and as armoured foot soldiers used battleaxes, spears and heavy two-handled swords to act as an impenetrable wall against the attack of enemy cavalry. Although they had horses they used them simply as transports to take them to the scene of the conflict, never engaging in formal cavalry actions.

Knockdoe lies near Lackagh, about half-way between Tuam to the north and Athenry to the south and eight miles north-east of Galway City. In a generally flat part of the county any rise would have been dignified by the title of *cnoc*. The battle was fought between the chief Norman-Irish leader Gearóid Mór Fitzgerald, 8th Earl of Kildare (1456-1513) and Ulick Burke, Earl of Clanrickarde who, although he had an obvious residual Norman name, regarded himself and his followers as Gaelic. He had become chieftain in 1485 and this meant that his followers were essentially, as in the description of Archdeacon John Lynch in 1662, *Hibernicis ipsis Hiberniores* ('More Irish than the Irish'). The battle was significant in that the 'English' Irish defeated the 'Irish' Irish and unwittingly tightened England's grip on the country. After the death of Henry VII in 1509 and of Gearóid himself four years later the field was open for Henry VIII to declare himself King of Ireland, as he did in 1541.

Those involved in the many intricate alliances of the battle could not have been aware of the far-reaching effects of the hosting call by the various chieftains. It must have seemed like another internecine conflict, like those characteristic of Ireland for centuries. The immediate source of the battle was Burke's territorial ambitions that had led him to occupy O'Kelly territory as a preliminary step towards assuming suzerainty over the whole of Connacht.

Conscious of Burke's refusal to acknowledge his sovereignty, Gearóid Mór had tried to ease tensions by marrying off his daughter Eustacia to him. He did not treat her particularly well and was living in open adultery with the wife of the O'Kelly, when he attacked and destroyed O'Kelly castles at Monivea, Garbally and Castleblakeney (all in east Galway and quite near to Knockdoe). Gearóid had no alternative in the light of such deliberate provocation but to lead an expedition against him. Gearóid's prime reason was to bring Burke back under obedience to Henry VII but he was also envious of his growing power in Connacht. The Kildare magnate remains an elusive and enigmatic figure; at this period in his life it is possible that he had the power completely to wrest Ireland away from England. Most of the Palesmen were under his control and he was connected by allegiance and marriage to the great northern tribes of MacMahon, O'Donnell and O'Neill, who would have followed him should he have decided to make the break.

Henry VII, an unemotional man with the mind of an accountant, wisely observed about Gearóid: 'He is meet to rule all Ireland seeing all Ireland cannot rule him.' The statement coolly included a tacit forgiveness for Gearóid's support of Richard III and his involvement in the conspiracies of Lambert Simnel and Perkin Warbeck. Kildare, perhaps conscious of the strength and determination of an England no longer weak because of the long-lasting Wars of the Roses, did not make any other treasonable moves but his son Gearóid Óg (1487-1534) and *his* son 'Silken Thomas (1513-37), the 10th Earl, died prisoners in the Tower of London, the latter hanged drawn and quartered on 3 February 1537. The Tudors had begun to make their intentions for Ireland more clear. They could not tolerate an independent Ireland, along with an independent Scotland. With countries so close in geographical terms as Ireland and Scotland, it was inevitable that one would try for hegemony over the others. The Tudors, sure of Welsh acquiescence, could not allow any further independence to the detached island to the west.

In the summer of 1504 these events were undreamed of. Kildare called upon all leal men to follow him and had the surprising support of the Burkes of Mayo as well as many of the northern Gaelic lords. The armies met to take part in the bloodiest civil battle in Irish history. Kildare's forces included many young Palesmen, supported by gallowglasses who were placed on the extreme right flank as they faced the Burke forces. The O'Kellys were also enthusiastic participants. Clanrickarde had persuaded (or compelled) the O'Briens of Thomond, the MacNamaras, the O'Kennedys and the O'Carrolls to follow him. He too had his supply of gallowglasses.

They fought on the lower slopes of the hill and along the banks of the River Clare that flows south on its circuitous route to Lough Corrib. Kildare's men in the centre were armed with 'bills', long battleaxes with concave blades. There were archers on both wings and Gearóid Óg, then only seventeen, commanded the reserve, frustrated that he was not in the 'battle' where most hand-to-hand fighting took place. Both sides had some armoured cavalry, diametrically opposite, left and right on the extreme wings as Kildare's army faced south-west. The reason for this unorthodox array was the existence of a little wall built across the battlefield by local farmers to guard their corn.

The battle raged all day and was, as usual, mainly a bill affair, although Burke's cavalry had an unusual piece of luck. They made a semicircular clockwise foray to Kildare's rear and fell upon some of the reserve force, who were guarding the 'luggage'. Aware that the battle had turned in favour of his father, Gearóid Óg had gone to join him and left only a few soldiers to guard the baggage. The Burke horsemen, thinking the battle over, began to collect the spoils. They soon learned that their main army was in rout. As the victors harried their retreating opponents they looted, burned enemy possessions and took prisoners, including two sons and a daughter of Ulick Burke, who may have been Kildare's own grandchildren. They were lucky, for out of the 6000 men on Kildare's side and 4000 on Burke's, perhaps a third died. Galway and the greater province were secured for the crown. It may have been the last pitched battle totally between Irishmen.

Farsetmore
8 May 1567

The battle of Farsetmore was fought and lost in the last year of the short, colourful life of Shane O'Neill (*c.* 1530-67), known to contemporaries and ever since as *Seán an Díomais* ('Shane the Proud'). He was the eldest legitimate son of Conn O'Neill (*c.* 1484-*c.* 1559), the 1st Earl of Tyrone, who had accepted the Tudor imposition of 'surrender and regrant', and as heir apparent declared himself to be the Ó Néill, assuming the Gaelic title of clan chieftainship. It was a bold move as there were other heirs presumptive and London had not yet recognised him as the second earl. By sheer force of personality, however, Shane persuaded the pragmatic Elizabeth I of his right to that title and in 1562 she greeted him speciously as such when he went on a diplomatic visit to her court. Farsetmore was fought against the other strong northern tribe and age-old enemy of the O'Neills, the O'Donnells, on their own territory in modern-day County Donegal. The new English lord deputy, Sir Henry Sidney (1529-86), an astute politician and one with a precise awareness of the Ulster situation, knew that the support of the O'Donnells was the best means of taming and finally bringing down the firebrand.

The O'Donnells had been a stable dynasty with father-son succession for a hundred years and in 1567 the chief was Hugh O'Donnell (a name that occurred regularly in the family). His chief stronghold was in Lifford in County Donegal, across the River Mourne from Strabane in present-day County Tyrone. With two strong clans living in close proximity dissension was almost inevitable, although they agreed to become allies to fight the Nine Years' War against the English later in the sixteenth century.

Anxious to assert his strength and independence, Hugh O'Donnell decided to take part in the current game of harassing Shane. He invaded O'Neill territory in the spring of 1567, crossing the river to lay waste the little town of Strabane and the fertile country around it. Safe in his own territory, he waited for Shane's next move. It came in the form of an army of around 2000 soldiers. Like the roughly equal force that came slowly out to meet them they consisted of the aristocracy, for whom warfare was a loyal duty, gallowglasses and the usual levy of able-bodied peasants who owed allegiance to O'Neill and served as cannon fodder. Shane's force moved west across the sandbank ford that gave Farsetmore its name – *Fearsaid Suilí*, its title in Irish, signifies 'Swilly sandbank'- for it is there that the River Swilly flows into the notoriously tidal lough of the same name. In later years colliers wishing to dock and unload at Letterkenny, less than a mile to the east, had to take the times of high tide into their calculations.

The reports of his scouts about the size of the army Shane was bringing against him startled Hugh O'Donnell at the beginning. He decided not to allow the O'Neill muster to advance too far into his territory but lacked the troops to prevent their incursion. He gathered what foot soldiers he could assemble and dispatched them to take the main thrust of the enemy, while messengers were sent all over his territories to look for reinforcements. In the meantime he sent his son, also called Hugh, with his cavalry in an eastern arc to meet Shane's, close to where the modern road runs to Ramelton. Young Hugh was unable to repel Shane's army but he managed to delay it long enough to allow his father to set up a defensive position in the boggy ground on the other side of the road. Eventually three different septs of the MacSwineys, the leading northern gallowglasses, arrived, making the two opposing forces approximately equal in numbers and arms. The O'Donnell mercenaries came swinging down from the north-west and the now combined forces arrayed to the north were more than able to withstand the attacks from the east. It cannot be proved but as they charged it is more than likely that the war cry 'Ó Dónaill Abú' was heard.

Hand-to-hand fighting occupied most of the day and then the O'Neill forces began to give way, vulnerable as they retreated to the merciless O'Donnell cavalry that was able to cover the perimeters of the field. As the foot soldiers withdrew they realised that the tide in the estuary was filling and that men and horses were drowning. It is likely that as many as 1300 of Shane's men were lost; the losses on the O'Donnell side were distinctly fewer. Two of Shane's grandsons, the MacDonald leader of his gallowglasses and Dualta Ó Donnaile, Shane's foster-brother, according to the annalists 'the person most faithful and dear to him in existence', were killed. Shane, shaken at how badly askew his plans had gone astray, escaped with his bodyguards along the north bank of the River Swilly to Scarrifhollis. Here he crossed the river and was guided to safety in Tyrone by the Gallaghers, who were traitors to the O'Donnells and well paid for their treachery. There was little left of the tough and politically astute man who had terrorised Ulster. In desperation he sought refuge with his former enemies, the MacDonnells of north Antrim but less than four weeks later he was murdered in Cushendall and his head taken to Dublin for spiking as an awful example to those who thought to outwit the Tudor machine.

GLENMALURE
25 AUGUST 1580

Glenmalure s a narrow valley, thirteen miles long, in the fastness of the Wicklow Mountains. It runs south-east from the Table Mountain to the Meeting of the Waters, the confluence of the rivers Avonmore and Avonbeg. The Avonbeg runs for most of its length. It is a trackless terrain susceptible to sudden mists – in fact an ideal country for guerrilla warfare. Towards the end of the sixteenth century it was O'Byrne territory and impossible to conquer by conventional means. Fiach Mac Aodh Ua Broin (anglicised as O'Byrne) (1544-97) maintained a fort at Ballincor in the glen and he could command at least a hundred expert swordsmen and many willing local fighters. His specific adversary was Arthur Grey, 14th Baron Grey de Wilton, who had been appointed Lord Deputy of Ireland in August 1580. With typical Tudor tunnel vision he assumed that it would be easy to rid the region of the outlaw who regularly caused damage to Dublin before returning to the safety of the Wicklow glens.

Grey had under his command 6000 men, freshly recruited, and he was determined to bring the terror of the Pale to heel before turning his attention to Munster and the Desmond rebellion. He headed west to enter County Wicklow through the plains of Kildare, then turned east, hoping to attack Ballincor from the Glen of Imaal. His conventional strategy was to drive O'Byrne's men headlong down the glen towards Avoca, where they could be dealt with by the English cavalry.

His men were dressed, as was the English custom, in their

brave scarlet and blue coats and as such made ideal targets for the concealed Irish, who had been equipped with unusually good firepower. The glen was overlooked on the south-west by Lugnaquilla (3039 ft), the highest peak in the Wicklow mountains, and by Lugaduff (2154 ft) on the north-east. Unless during one of the county's famous mists, scouts on either peak would be able to track any movement of troops.

The veteran officers in Grey's army advised strongly against the plan of campaign but the only compromise the Lord Deputy would make was to use half of his force and keep 3000 men in reserve. Lookouts at the summit of Lugnaquilla saw the incursion, not that any of Grey's forces tried to conceal their presence. They stumbled down in full dress regalia to the sound of drums. (The psychology seems to have been that the panoply of real soldiers and martial music would terrify the near-savage Irish.) When they reached the depths of Glenmalure they found not a serviceable road but the swift-flowing Avonbeg. Immediately O'Byrne's snipers found their targets, easily decimating the gaudily clad troopers as they prepared for close battle. They turned and ran headlong down the valley only to meet with O'Byrne's kerne (*ceithearn*) the fast-moving Irish mercenary band, expert in hand-to-hand encounters, who did as much damage with swords, spears and axes as the musketeers did with their flintlocks. Grey sent out his cavalry not to mop up the fleeing Irish, as he had intended, but to try to stiffen his own infantry's resistance, as many of the soldiers in their retreat had thrown away their weapons. The reserve had to fight a strong rearguard action as they withdrew towards the town of Rathdrum.

THE NINE YEARS' WAR 1594-1603

CLONTIBRET
25-27 MARCH 1595

Located in County Monaghan, Clontibret, on the modern N2, is taken as being the half-way point between Derry and Dublin. It was the first battle in the Nine Years' War in which Hugh O'Neill (*c.* 1550-1616), 2nd Earl of Tyrone, known to his contemporaries simply as 'Tyrone' and to later biographers as the 'Great O'Neill', was formally involved. The state of belligerence with England had its origins in the actions of Lord Deputy Fitzwilliam in partitioning MacMahon land in Monaghan and executing Hugh Roe, the head of the clan, on the grounds of his breaking the terms of his 'surrender and regrant' agreement. This was a supposed attempt at the reconciling of the Gaelic system of aristocracy and rule with that of Britain but accurately seen by the astute O'Neill as a first step towards a total Tudor domination of the island.

In earlier confrontations, notably the battle of the 'Ford of the Biscuits', when, on 7 August 1594, a column on its way to relieve the fort at Enniskillen was turned back by a combined force led by Red Hugh O'Donnell (1572-1602), Cormac O'Neill (Hugh's brother) and Maguire of Fermanagh, there was no material proof of Hugh O'Neill's involvement but his was the tactical skill that gave the Irish the edge in many engagements. The battle's colourful name arose from the food supplies that were lost while the column tried to ford the river Arney between Upper and Lower Lough Erne in Fermanagh. Although O'Neill disclaimed all knowledge of complicity he arrived two days later to collect booty and obtain an estimate of English strength.

Like most of O'Neill's encounters with Tudor forces during the Nine Years' War, the battle of Clontibret had a strong element of ambush about it. The engagement was with the army of Sir Henry Bagenal (c. 1556-1598), O'Neill's brother-in-law through his marriage to Mabel Bagenal. Bagenal's relief column from Dundalk was attacked on its way to and from Monaghan fort. The soldiers were engaged by the Irish soldiers of O'Neill and O'Donnell, supplemented by 'Redshanks' (mercenaries from the Highlands and Islands of Scotland, who wore kilts), at Crossdall, four miles from their goal. At 4000 the Irish army greatly outnumbered Bagenal's force of 1750. They were deployed among the bogs and thickets and, using caliver muskets, killed twelve and wounded thirty of Bagenal's men but made no attempt at hand-to-hand fighting. Bagenal reached Monaghan on the evening of 25 March. He left one company in the town and, worried about his supply of powder and ball, decided to return to Dundalk, his base, by a safer route via Newry. He took a day's rest and left for Dundalk on 27 March. At Clontibret, Bagenal marched into a similar ambush in drumlin country, designed as if by nature for that kind of fighting.

Again musket fire was heavy and escape was made difficult by O'Neill's cavalry, who circled the perimeter of the battlefield. One of Bagenal's cavalry commanders, a Palesman called Seagrave, decided that a charge against the Irish was the only hope of preventing a massacre. Seagrave found himself in close personal combat with O'Neill. Tyrone's standard bearer cut off Seagrave's arm and O'Neill finished the work with a dagger wound in the groin. At nightfall Bagenal prepared to make some kind of stand against the Irish push he expected. That it did not come was probably due to O'Neill own lack of powder and an instinctive reluctance to risk a pitched battle. Bagenal was thus able to hold on until help arrived from Newry.

For the first time O'Neill's hand was shown; until then he could behave as a liege lord to Elizabeth I (1558-1603), Her Majesty's Earl of Tyrone, even offering help and advice to the English forces. With his Pale upbringing and acquaintance with Tudor realpolitik

O'Neill knew Elizabeth's ultimate goal and he suspected correctly that he was Ireland's last hope of halting total conquest. He, unlike the other Irish earls, was cool-headed, except on rare and usually disastrous occasions. He used a period of wary détente with England to build up Irish resistance and train his armies in modern weapons. The instinctive swordsmen were taught to use the fairly accurate calivers by frequent practice with targets and so far as possible the foot soldiers were shown how to use the local terrain to increase the efficiency of their ambushes. The English, noting the prevalence of this kind of attack, made the mistake of thinking that it was because of cowardice on the part of the Irish. They were all the more discomfited to discover that when it came to close fighting – 'push of pike' as they called it – the Irish were ferociously brave and deadly in action.

Clontibret was more than just a tactical setback for Elizabeth's men; it hurt her in prestige and was wearyingly costly. Only the fear of the near proximity of Ireland, a country mainly Catholic and Hispanophile, a convenient lateral conduit for the dreaded Counter-Reformation to spread from Spain, kept the queen from relinquishing her territorial claim. She dreaded most the capacity of O'Neill for uniting the riven north, his combination of logistical skill and charismatic leadership. The Nine Years' War was nearly won by the Irish, except that England's preternatural good luck held. 'God's wind' blew and scattered the Spanish Armada in 1588 and in spite of O'Neill's mastery of tactics he eventually failed to persuade the Old English Catholics to side with him against the queen.

CARRICKFERGUS
4 NOVEMBER 1597

In the turbulence of the Nine Years' War, Scots and Irish often united against the common foe and the English garrison at Carrickfergus was attacked several times by Scots soldiers under various MacDonnell chiefs. The grim, near-impregnable keep built by John de Courcy in 1178 had been occupied after several attempts by Edward Bruce and the Chichester family used it as their military base

The Chichesters had been granted land in Antrim and Down, with an element of 'plantation by stealth' to add to the original grant. Arthur Chichester (1563-1625) was to become the main pursuant of the Ulster planation and spur to Imeacht na nIarlaí, the so-called 'Flight of the Earls' in 1609. The Clandeboye O'Neills (Clann Aodh Bhuí) were usually at enmity with Sir John Chichester, Arthur's elder brother and the custodian of Carrickfergus. Sorley Boy MacDonnell (c. 1505-90) had sacked the town in 1575 in vengeance for the massacre of his family on Rathlin Island carried out by Walter Devereux, 1st Earl of Essex, who gave orders for a similar punitive expedition against Clandeboye. Now, in 1597, Sorley Boy's nephew, James MacSorley MacDonnell, led a mixed army of Irish and Scots to meet Sir John Chichester, to discuss his attacks on the Clandeboye O'Neills.

A force of 1800, made up of 1300 Irish and 500 trained Scots musket men, was rather a large party to take to the parley arranged for 4 November. The MacDonnell forces chose a spot four miles north-east of Carrickfergus along the northern shore of

Belfast Lough. When Chichester saw the extent of MacDonnell's army he felt it advisable to put on an equivalent show of force, consisting of five companies of foot and one of cavalry. There was an impasse as each side eyed the other and then without warning, Chichester unwisely gave the order to his horse to charge. The Scots fell back into the hills and Chichester, with a small number of troopers, found himself isolated. The Scots regrouped and charged, wounding Chichester in the leg. He remounted and led a counter-charge with his remaining soldiers from the small rise where he and his cavalry were drawn up. He was shot in the head and killed instantaneously. His troops scattered, some making for Larne Lough and escaping into Island Magee, swimming or floating their horses across. As in other battles in the off-on war the English were startled by the scarlet coats of the Scots musketeers; camouflage did not count for much in the formal battles of the day.

Chichester's forces, now leaderless and reckoned to number no more than 350 men in total, had to contend with a much greater number of fresh soldiers. They had not been rested after their foray and were short of powder. 180 of them were killed and thirty wounded. Chichester's head was hacked off his shoulders and taken as a trophy to O'Neill's camp in Dungannon, where it was used as a football. The English Privy Council was not especially shocked by this piece of barbarity – it was a raw time – and blamed the débâcle on Chichester's 'own hazarding' but his younger brother, the adventurous Arthur, essentially the founder of Protestant Ulster, determined to avenge his brother's death. The prospect of revenge coupled with profit seemed attractive to this typical Tudor adventurer; the bringing down of the Earl of Tyrone was merely the icing on the cake.

From England's point of view Carrickfergus was another inexplicable defeat and although O'Neill was not directly involved he began to assume in Tudor eyes the persona of the great Satan, a dangerous because clever adversary, controlling from his castle in Dungannon every nefarious action against the Queen's majesty.

THE YELLOW (BLACKWATER) FORD
14 AUGUST 1598

The boundary between the modern counties of Tyrone and Armagh is the River Blackwater which flows in a leisurely zigzag from County Monaghan until it reaches Lough Neagh at Coney Island. It had proved to be a problematic boundary for Tudor and earlier armies in their long drawn-out struggles with the native Irish. Armagh city, like most of the Ulster towns, had served as a garrison from Norman times. The territory of the Earl of Tyrone, Hugh O'Neill (*c.* 1550-1516), lay north and west of the town of Armagh, now ruined by frequent attacks by O'Neill's forces, so the building of an advance fort by the English commanders as close as safety permitted to the enemy's ground was not only advisable but essential.

The Blackwater fort, replacing one destroyed by O'Neill in 1595, was built at Portmore, five miles north-west of Armagh, and almost immediately it became a target for him. Tactically the building of the fort seemed a good idea as it was relatively easy for the English to observe enemy territory from it, but in its isolation it was vulnerable to native attack, although the river was deep and wide at that point.

It was this construction that ended a period of relative peace in Ulster since the battle of Clontibret more than three years previously. O'Neill, who had no lack of men, knew the terrain and could live off the land, determined to sack this fort also. It took him a very short time to surround it, although several attempts at capture were violently repulsed.

Portmore was well fortified but by the summer of 1598, supplies of food and arms were running low. The viceroy, Lord Burgh, who had ordered is construction in the first place, insisted that it should be maintained and although he had died of the fever in October 1597 his policies were retained by his successors. Sir Henry Bagenal (c. 1556-1598), perhaps unwisely, volunteered to command the relief party. It was he who had advised Burgh of the need to keep up pressure on O'Neill. He was still smarting from his defeat at Clontibret and his long personal animus against O'Neill was made more bitter by the death in 1596 of his sister Mabel, who had married O'Neill against his wishes. The slur of Henry Bagenal's refusing Mabel a dowry had made the hatred mutual and when she had left her husband because of his multiple infidelity and returned in shame to Newry, the Bagenal home, an extra dimension of rancour was added to the relationship.

Portmore was, in modern parlance, a fort too far. The terrain was thickly wooded where it was not boggy and it was home ground to O'Neill's own army, although perhaps not so familiar to his formidable allies, Red Hugh O'Donnell from Tír Chonaill (Donegal) and Maguire of Fermanagh. In preparation for the battle O'Neill had his engineers dig trenches along and across the road from Armagh to the fort. The deepest and best trench, furnished with sharpened stakes, was constructed between two little hills sited about half-way between the Blackwater River and the Callan River that flows from Armagh. It was about a mile long, four feet wide and five feet deep and was topped on both sides with a thickset thorny hedge, the contemporary equivalent of barbed-wire entanglements.

Bagenal was confident that in a pitched battle his troops could overcome the motley collection of the Irish and Scots that would oppose them. He had been born in Newry and in previous engagements had become well-acquainted with the Armagh terrain. His troops marched with trumpets, horns and drums sounding, with the intention of unnerving the superstitious natives. There were about 3500 foot and 350 cavalry in the crown army and they were to face an enemy equally numerous and one that had a greater stake in the outcome. Inspired by their clan chiefs, the army of O'Neill and his allies had a sense of the possibility of defeating the foreigner and shoring up the crumbling fabric of the Gaelic order.

Bagenal divided his foot soldiers into six striking divisions, with two as vanguard, two in the centre and two in the rear. Cavalry protected the wings. It was possibly a mixture of bravado and the desire to inspire his men that made Bagenal march with the leading company and this decision proved disastrous: he fell early, shot through the head. It was a serious blow not only to morale but to the control of the troops that the 'marshal', as commanders-in-chief were called, was dead. Sir Thomas Maria Wingfield, his second-in-command, was in charge of veteran troops seasoned by campaigns in Brittany. He continued to march towards the Blackwater fort, determined to carry out Bagenal's (and Burgh's) intention. The English troops were now being attacked from both sides and another accident caused by an artillery match detonated their store of powder. Their artillery superiority meant very little without powder and their prime cannon, a saker (of French manufacture) became stuck in the yellow mud that gave the place its name. (The exact location of the battle known by name to every Irish child has never been precisely marked; there was no ford of that name and it probably described the muddy terrain between the little hills and the thickets.)

Wingfield wisely ordered a retreat but Evans, who commanded the vanguard, did not comply, either because he refused or, more likely had not received the order. The result was that his men were confused and awkwardly compressed. O'Neill first sent his cavalry against them to break their formation and followed with his pikemen and sabremen who, although suffering inevitable losses in the close fighting, killed hundreds of the forces of the Crown. It is thought that about three hundred of the Ulster army died. The survivors harried the enemy all the way back to Armagh, the English flanks pinned in by the Irish horsemen and by the hidden musketeers. The English cavalry made no attempt to engage the ferocious Irish but left the field, making for the safety of Armagh, where the English base camp had been established. There were also about 900 desertions from the crown troops – a number were themselves Irish – who either made their way to their homes or who joined the Irish side. The wounded who were left behind on the field were finished off, there being no arrangements for prisoners. About nine hundred of Bagenal's army died, including eighteen officers, and the rest found that they were unable to leave Armagh, which then showed obvious signs of the attacks.

O'Neill had won a famous victory and the terms for parley were severe. Safe passage to Newry of the remnants of Bagenal's army was guaranteed after surrender of all arms and ammunition. There they were allowed to board ships that would take them to Dublin. Portmore was abandoned. Although it would greatly increase the cost of the war Elizabeth's advisers urged the building up of English military strength in Ireland. O'Neill was at the height of his powers and many leaders, hitherto neutral or quiescent, began to support his rebellion. The unfortunate death of Philip II (1527-98) and the succession of his indolent and irresolute son Philip III (1578-1621) prevented O'Neill from maximising his opportunity and establishing a firm compact with Spain that could have allowed him to obtain a kind of independence for Ireland.

CAHIR CASTLE
26-29 MAY 1599

Robert Devereux (1566-1601), 2nd Earl of Essex, a likely lover of Elizabeth I, proved a better courtier than a general. Famous as the man whose ears were boxed by the queen for turning his back on her and as the author of an attempted coup on 8 February 1601, he was executed for treason shortly after its failure. He was never very successful as a commander but continually forgiven by the queen until his 'failure' in Ireland – the result of the treaty he made with Hugh O'Neill and his refusal to carry out the queen's orders.

Essex arrived in the country the spring of 1599 with the largest army ever to land in Ireland (16,000 men and 1300 horse) but ignored Ulster and headed for Munster to defend the province from a possible Spanish invasion. His wastefulness and arrogance in dubbing his colleagues knights without royal assent was a constant source of chagrin to Elizabeth, who had a better grasp of Irish affairs at home in Westminster than Essex had *in situ*. She was unimpressed by his refusal to engage with O'Neill but wearily acquiesced as he headed for the quieter south-west.

Cahir Castle, built in the 12th century by the O'Briens on a rock in the River Suir, gave its name to the present-day town in County Tipperary. It was regarded by the English as a source of treason, 'a bulwark for Munster and a safe retreat for all the agents of Spain and Rome'. As such it was a significant prize, tactically and symbolically, and it was believed that possession of it was necessary for control of the south-west. It was owned by Lord Cahir, an Irish aristocrat loyal to Elizabeth but custodian James

Galdie, Cahir's brother, was not reliable. Also involved in its history was Edward Fitzgibbon (c. 1552-1608), the hereditary White Knight whose public support of the English was never quite complete, and who was consequently regarded as unreliable by both sides.

Essex assembled his army in Clonmel, about ten miles to the east, on 25 May 1599. There were three divisions, the middle division responsible for dragging Essex's artillery by hand. Draught horses should have been requisitioned but the firepower, a heavy cannon and a culverin, a firepiece notable for its long barrel, had come up-river from Waterford. Lord Cahir, who accompanied Essex, promised that Galdie would surrender the castle without a fight. He went ahead, accompanied by Henry Danvers, Essex's commander of horse, but failed in his effort to gain control of the castle and was immediately accused by the mercurial Essex of bad faith.

Essex was now determined to capture the castle himself. He and Colonel George Bingham, who had been successful against the Maguires' stronghold in Enniskillen five years earlier, worked out a plan of urgent attack. There were fears of a rebel army in the vicinity and in the rainy summer there were greater fears of typhus. Essex's army used natural ditches and remains of old walls on the castle's east side to construct an artillery platform that could take the weight of the cannons. The engineers used gabions, wicker baskets filled with earth and small stones, as base and arranged for the culverin to be set further back because of its longer range. Three hundred men were sent to occupy the outbuildings on the south side, although it required a dangerous passage across a kind of causeway made of woven osiers across a tributary stream.

By the morning of 27 May, Pentecost Sunday, the cannon were ready, their barrels trained upon the hitherto impregnable citadel. The second ball from the one of the cannon had such a recoil that its mounting was fractured and the repairs took a day and a half. The culverin did much greater damage after the first shell was dislodged from its long barrel. Fifty effective shots were fired at the east façade of the castle. Meanwhile the White Knight had entered the castle by the west entrance and allowed those unfit to defend to leave (the White Knight was friendly towards the Irish). Essex, scenting success, caused two bridges that connected the castle to the west bank to be destroyed. That evening both guns were made ready for firing, the culverin being moved closer.

On the Monday morning the bombardment began again and this time the east wall was breached and Essex's highly efficient engineers began constructing equipment for assault: ladders, scaffolding and protective screens. Petards, an early form of grenade, were prepared for demolishing heavy doors and other obstructions. A kind of mole trench was built from the river bank so that the foot soldiers could occupy the castle as soon as the engineers had done their work.

Instead of suing for peace the members of the garrison tried to slip away during the night but they were spotted by a company of Flanders veterans and eighty were killed as they tried to come out of the river. Essex's troops met no resistance as they occupied the fort. The gaps in the walls were soon mended and before he withdrew Essex left a garrison of a hundred men under George Carey, who died soon after from a face wound sustained in the fighting. Galdie and some of his officers managed to escape through a sink shaft under a watermill.

Essex hoped to add Cahir to his list of battle honours, to become a hero of Desmond as well as Cadiz, but the queen was not impressed. His meeting with O'Neill at the ford of Bellaclinthe in Louth the following September and the ceasefire that followed ended his credibility as a commander and he shortly returned to England.

CURLEW PASS
15 AUGUST 1599

The battle of the Curlew Pass between Red Hugh O'Donnell (1572-1602), and Sir Conyers Clifford in the Curlew Mountains north of Boyle, County Roscommon. As changing allegiances among the Irish were as characteristic of this period as they had been of earlier centuries, the English, especially the Earl of Essex (1566-1601), tried to use old enmities to weaken O'Neill and his allies. Donough O'Connor, an Irish chieftain from Sligo, seized the opportunity to expel O'Donnell's forces from the land that they had occupied and agreed to aid an English attack on the Lord of Tír Chonaill. Essex realised the advantage of holding Ballyshannon, only twenty miles from Sligo and providing a convenient entrée into the north-west O'Donnell territories. *Tibóid na Long* ('Theobald of the Ships') Burke (the son of the 'pirate queen' Granuaile), who was loyal to the queen, was appointed as joint commander with an English captain. They were to sail to Sligo and rendezvous with O'Connor in Sligo Bay.

O'Donnell's sources of intelligence were excellent and he was able to send a force of more than 2000 to Collooney Castle in County Sligo, O'Connor's northern stronghold, with instructions to starve him into surrender. Essex's commander in Athlone, the nearest garrison to Collooney, was the relatively experienced Conyers Clifford and Essex ordered him to relieve the castle. Essex saw the move as a diversionary tactic to weaken O'Neill's power of resistance in Ulster and as such, considered it a worthwhile enterprise.

It was a distance of forty-five miles from Athlone to the Curlew Mountains and a further twenty-two to Collooney. The weather was hot and Clifford, in his urgency to engage with O'Donnell's forces, marched his own troops inadvisedly fast. They were fatigued and undersupplied with food, as his commissariat officers warned him, but he kept up their spirits with promises of meat at the end of the battle. His scouts had assured him that the pass through the Curlews was undefended and he was logistically certain that with 1500 foot and two hundred horse he could easily subdue the besieging force on the wide plain on the other side of the mountains. Clifford's army marched with full panoply through Roscommon, Tulsk and Boyle, bristling with spears and war standards.

O'Donnell, using the same successful tactics as O'Neill had done elsewhere, prepared a series of ambush sites along the route through the hills. Trees were felled, trenches dug and the main body of his infantry were held just out of sight beyond the ridge of the mountains. The Irish skirmishers lined the pass, well-equipped with arrows, javelins and muskets. There were also men trained with slingshots and others who could inflict lethal damage with fist-sized rocks. O'Donnell had left only three hundred of the forces besieging Collooney with his cousin Niall Garbh and sent the rest east towards Sligo to prevent Clifford's relief forces from sailing into Sligo Bay. (Niall Garbh was afterwards accused of betraying O'Donnell.)

Clifford's forces met the first obstacle when they began to climb the hills. At 860 feet they were not hard to scale but the afternoon of 15 August was blisteringly hot. The soldiers managed to force their way through and confidently headed further up the hills. Woodland and bog on both sides gave excellent cover and the more seasoned English officers could not get rid of the sensation of moving more deeply into a trap.

When Clifford's advance troops had marched a considerable distance into the hills a bitter firefight followed. The Irish troops, well-fed and rested, effectively terrified the weary, hungry English, who, ignoring their officers, began to slip away from the fight. Those who stayed ran out of powder after ninety minutes and it was then that they met the full force of the main body of the Irish soldiers. The resulting close battle caused many of the English to turn and head back down the hills, causing great confusion among the main column; most of them joined in the race towards Boyle. It was no territory for cavalry but the English flankers did their best to protect the fleeing foot soldiers. In a desperate attempt to stiffen resistance, Clifford ordered some of his men to join him in a charge but he was almost immediately run through the chest by an Irish pike. Reaching level ground again, the cavalry drew themselves up in two protective flanks, allowing the main body of demoralised infantry to reach Boyle and seek refuge in the abbey in the town.

In accordance with the barbaric practice of the time Clifford was decapitated and the head sent to O'Donnell. Conor MacDermott, a local chieftain who had joined forces with O'Donnell, secured Clifford's body, intending to use it as a bargaining tool for the recovery of some of his men who were being held prisoner by the English. The body was eventually buried in the monastery in Boyle. It was another victory for the Irish and one of the causes of Essex's agreeing to a truce with O'Neill. It is also remembered for the participation of Brian Óg O'Rourke of Breffni, another chieftain on the side of O'Donnell, whose warlike exploits had earned him the soubriquet, 'Brian of the Battleaxes'. The battle of Curlew Pass is commemorated at the scene by a representative statue entitled 'The Gaelic Chieftain' by the Derry sculptor Maurice Harron. It was unveiled in 1999, the four-hundredth anniversary of the battle.

MOYRY PASS
20 SEPTEMBER-9 OCTOBER 1600

The Moyry Pass (*Bealach na Mhaigre*='the way of the salmon')
is also known as the 'Gap of the North' and its potential military
difficulties can easily be appreciated by the train traveller from
Dublin to Belfast. Ben Kiely called it 'mystic country, fairy
country', with strong folk memories of Cú Chulainn. Between
Dundalk and Newry the local topography leaves a narrow pass
between Slieve Gullion and Camlough Mountain and at the
beginning of seventeenth century this was the most convenient
entrance to unruly Ulster, still largely unaffected by all the earlier
conquests. To the south and east lay the safe ground of the loyal
Pale and it was from here that the new Lord Deputy, Charles
Blount, 8th Baron Mountjoy (1563-1606), began his campaign
against Hugh O'Neill (*c*. 1550-1516), Earl of Tyrone and Lord of
Ulster. He was a close friend of the Earl of Essex (1566-1601) and
determined to succeed where his friend had failed. Loyal to the
queen, he wished to impose, as King James I (1566-1625) would
later put it, English 'civility' upon the wild Irish and knew that
O'Neill was the main obstacle to that desirable aim.

Mountjoy's method was the same as his predecessor, Lord
Burgh's: to establish garrisons in central and western Ulster and
from there eventually to control the last serious opposition to the
English queen. The complex of drumlins, bog, thicket and lake
stretching from Carlingford Lough in the east to Donegal Bay had
been for centuries an effective barrier for the Ulster territories
and the Moyry Pass the safest and most obvious portal from the

south. Derry and Carrickfergus, both safe harbours, were also to play their part in Mountjoy's grand design. The Moyry Pass was less a pitched battle than a lengthy campaign, and one fought in abysmal Irish weather, with torrential rain, hurricane winds and thick fog to add to his soldiers' discomfort.

Mountjoy left Dundalk on 17 September 1600 and headed for Newry, en route for Armagh. His intention was to recommission the ruinous fort at Armagh, effectively lost after Bagenal's defeat at the Yellow Ford the previous winter. The forces of Hugh O'Neill were now becoming adept at the trick of defensive trench-building and the effective technique of 'plashing': forming a wickerwork of sallies and other pliable branches to make an effective barrier and stop the English forces from occupying the heights on both sides of the pass. O'Neill had his men construct three defensive trenches with spiked-topped palisades across the only road through the pass, which was described by one of the English officers as, 'a broken causey beset on both sides with bogs, where the Irish might skip but the English could not go'. (It was information like this from the front describing the O'Neill tactic of sharp attack and even sharper withdrawal that enabled Shakespeare to speak of 'skipping kernes' in *Macbeth*, which was written a few years later. Kern (Irish *ceithearnach*) was a general name for a lightly-armed Irish foot soldier.) Another successful new tactic that seemed to enrage the English out of all proportion was the verbal onslaught practised by advance parties of the Irish; they were supremely successful at prompted frontline vituperation: whether they realised the full significance of calling their enemies 'churls' is nor clear but it certainly enraged them.

On 2 October Sir Samuel Bagnall, at Mountjoy's command, led a force of five regiments into the pass. The heavy rain of the previous six days during which the matchlock muskets could not be used, had given way to a thick mist. Bagnall's forces breached the first trench and made for the second and third only to discover that they were now being fired on from both sides of the plashed thickets and from the head of the pass. After a toll of forty-six dead and 120 wounded the English withdrew to their main camp on Faughart Hill (see page 44), where Edward Bruce had been killed. Three days later, Mountjoy tried to outflank the Irish by sending a force of two regiments round the hills to the west of the pass while another regiment attempted to force a way through the centre. Again the flankers faced a close hand-to-hand struggle and were forced to withdraw, while no progress at all was reported along the 'causey'. This time the toll was fifty men dead and 200 wounded.

Mountjoy withdrew entirely to Faughart and sat down to wait. He was conscious that after nearly three weeks of intense skirmishing his adversary must by now be short of powder, and more, seriously of food. On 14 October his scouts were able to tell him that O'Neill had withdrawn completely from Moyry and retreated to his crannóg fort on Lough Lurcan, between Newry and Armagh. (Crannógs, usually artificial islands on lakes, had been used as strongholds and refuges from pre-Celtic times. The causeways connecting them to the lough shore were easily destroyed in emergencies.)

Mountjoy's forces advanced warily through the empty pass on 17 October, dismantling the earthworks as they went. He did not dare to attempt to fortify Armagh but was content to build a primitive fort at Mount Norris, half-way between Newry and the ecclesiastical capital. The battle was a draw, neither side able to claim a victory, but with a greatly inflated tally of dead Irish, Mountjoy was able to give Queen Elizabeth some heart.

KINSALE
24 DECEMBER 1601

The battle that marked the end of Ireland's hope of at least a temporary independence lasted barely three hours. It was the climax of the 16th-century Irish rebellion, popularly known as the Nine Years' War, that had Hugh O'Neill (c. 1550-1616) recognised as unquestionably the lord of Gaelic Ulster and a possible prince of a separate Ireland; it would have been a step too far to think of the title of sovereign as Henry VIII (1491-1547) had already declared himself king of Ireland in 1541. Until Kinsale, O'Neill had shown himself a superb commander in a series of successful engagements, using the unorthodox fighting talents of his clansmen and those of his Ulster allies, especially the followers of Red Hugh O'Donnell (1572-1602), the Lord of Tír Chonaill, and reserving to himself the choice of location. The running sore of Ulster was playing havoc with the Tudor exchequer and no sovereign was quite so conscious of cost as Elizabeth I (1558-1603). Now events forced O'Neill, with obvious reluctance, to fight three hundred miles from his home, the terrain and timing not of his choosing.

The struggle with the convenient title of 'Nine Years' War' occurred in a country intermittently at peace and one in which many of the population were unaffected at first: in later years the 'scorched earth' policy of both sides caused grievous famine. Now, in the first year of the new century the coming of the long-promised troops from Spain brought a fresh urgency to the situation. As on earlier and later occasions, events in Ireland were merely a part of a wider European conflict. Philip III of Spain (1578-1621) wanted a diversionary action to take some of the heat out of his war in the Netherlands. This, rather than any sense of being the military arm of the Counter-Reformation, was his main motive in 'helping' O'Neill.

Of many possible landfalls for the Spanish troops grudgingly dispatched by Philip, Kinsale was the least satisfactory but weather, as ever, played its part in the decision to land at the little port on the Bandon River. As it was, gales off the south coast of Spain had driven eight of the galleons back to Cádiz, unfortunately those with the gunpowder and the 2000 more experienced soldiers. The 4000 who landed in Kinsale on 2 October 1601 (because the revised Gregorian calender was not adopted in England until 1752) at once occupied the town and withstood a siege by O'Neill's old enemy Mountjoy, who had mobilised as large an army as he dared from garrisons of the Pale.

O'Neill wasted no time but gathered a large army that eventually camped north of the town at Coolcarron. The combined armies of the Irish amounted to 6000 troops, mainly of infantry with some light cavalry. Mountjoy's encampment, due south of Coolcarron, was riddled with dysentery and, because of a blockade organised efficiently by O'Neill's allies, extremely short of rations. O'Neill's instinctive reaction would have been to sit and let disease and hunger do his work for him but for reasons not exactly clear he was finally persuaded to end his usual defensive stance and engage in a full-frontal attack. The usual reason given was that the younger Hugh O'Donnell, impetuous and weary of the attrition of maintaining the siege, persuaded him to risk a 'field'.

O'Donnell's impatience at the delay in attack was partly caused by a sense of insecurity at being so many hundreds of miles from his territories in the north-west. His success in keeping an effective army under control after a remarkable journey of 250 miles from his castle in Lifford to the very south of the country – a journey for a venturesome crow but much longer for O'Donnell as he force-marched his army over bleak, wintry, trackless territory at the mercy of disease and lack of provisions, while running the risk of subsidiary battles – was prodigious. He had mustered his men in Ballymote, County Sligo, on 2 November and marched south through Roscommon and east Galway, gathering followers from Connacht clans as he went along. He drove his men over the Slieve Phelim mountains, fifteen miles east of Limerick, to avoid attack from Sir George Carew (1555-1629), the Tudor Lord of Munster, who had intended to block his passage at Cashel. The mountains were covered with snow and ice and the O'Donnell forces were made to cover forty miles a day, a pace that Carew could not match.

An open confrontation was not as risky a plan as it might have seemed. The Irish had shown themselves perfectly capable of a conventional clash of might in short bursts at the Yellow Ford and the Moyry Pass. The date chosen for the battle was Christmas Eve. Security was weak and the English seemed to have prior knowledge of the Irish attack. Because of delay in formation, what had been intended as a night battle was delayed until a bitter December morning. For some reason neither O'Donnell nor Don Aguila, the Spanish general, advanced at the agreed moment and the result was that O'Neill's infantry had to face the most experienced of Mountjoy's troops without reinforcements. As his troops began to give way, O'Neill ordered them to retreat to the kind of boggy land that had suited them in the past but Mountjoy's highly trained cavalry drove them headlong and essentially routed them. The lighter Irish horsemen, with less armour and often without stirrups, were unable to stop their charge and as they, too, took flight, they scattered their own foot soldiers. As was customary in armies gathered from untrained tenants, many took the opportunity to desert and the sight of the headlong race of O'Neill's infantry was enough to dispirit O'Donnell's army, who also began a withdrawal back home to Ulster. The Spaniards under Don Juan del Águila were able to sue for peace on reasonable terms a few weeks later.

Although not the end of the war, nor indeed of O'Neill's career as a Gaelic leader, the battle of Kinsale was the ultimate lost opportunity and as such has attained a special place in the sentimental mythology of popular Irish history. The terms of settlement at Mellifont in 1603 would, say a decade earlier, have satisfied O'Neill. His sudden leaving of Ulster with his aristocratic companions in 1607, a departure injudiciously called the 'Flight of the Earls', may have been part of a long-term strategy to return with an army strong enough to oust the English once for all. The emotionally unloaded Irish word *imeacht* ('departing') used by the chroniclers better conveys the nature of the leaving of Hugh O'Neill and others.

The sense of a never-to-be-repeated chance lost has caused the accretion of myths about the event and it holds its share of epic deeds. Red Hugh O'Donnell, O'Neill's late rival and fiery younger second-in-command, lived on in history and myth not only because of his epic march to Kinsale but because of his adventurous earlier escapades, such as escaping from Dublin Castle at the age of nineteen after an incarceration of four years After Kinsale he left for Spain, perhaps hoping, like O'Neill, to return with a larger army to drive the Tudors at last from Ireland. Before the end of 1602 he was dead in Simancas, just thirty years of age – poisoned, it was believed, by a British agent. But this too may have been part of the Red Hugh myth

The Siege of Dunboy
5-18 June 1602

Dunboy Castle is situated near the town of Castletownbere on the south coast of the Beara peninsula in County Cork. It was built as a defensive keep to overlook the harbour of Bearhaven, part of the sea lough of Bantry Bay, and was the stronghold of Dónal Cam O'Sullivan Beare (1560-1616), the local clan leader, known as the 'Chief of Dunboy'. The Irish epithet *cam* ('twisted') probably referred to a wry neck, the result of an old wound. Dónal Cam had early responded to O'Neill's campaign to oust the Tudors. Dismayed by the defeat at Kinsale, the retreat of O'Neill to Ulster, the hasty departure of O'Donnell to Spain and the withdrawal of the Spanish forces under Águila, he determined to continue the struggle. Dunboy had been occupied by a small force of Spaniards under Captain Saavedra, who were preparing to hand it over to Sir George Carew (1555-1629), Lord President of Munster. O'Sullivan overcame that garrison without much difficulty and released the strangers unharmed to return to Spain. He kept their arms and powder for his own use and left a force of 143 of his best soldiers to guard the castle while he moved to another of his fortresses, Ardea Castle, on the north coast of the peninsula, overlooking the Kenmare River.

Carew was determined to crush all opposition to the queen and advanced with a force of 5000 men and much heavy artillery. They began a severe bombardment both on land and from Bantry Bay. The rocky fort seemed impregnable until Owen O'Sullivan, one of Donal's cousins, informed Carew that one part of the walls of Dunboy, located over a stairwell, was weaker than the rest. After a relentless battering it became clear by the tenth day that the fort was about to fall. Richard MacGeoghan, who had been left as commander by O'Sullivan, sent a messenger to Carew to ask for surrender terms. The Lord of Munster responded in a fashion characteristic of the time and of Tudor absoluteness by hanging the poor messenger in full sight of the defenders. With more hope than confidence, most of them slid into the water below the keep and tried to swim to Beare Island. Many perished and the rest were taken prisoner. The castle fell the next day; the rearguard force were winkled out of the cellar, although not before they had attempted to blow up their remaining store of gunpowder. Most were hanged in the market-square of Castletown Berehaven. Friar Dominic Collins, who had stayed in Dunboy, was tortured in the hope that before his execution he would renounce his Papism but he stayed steadfast and was later hanged in Youghal.

During the siege Carew had sought out O'Sullivan families on Dursey Island off the tip of the Beara peninsula and engaged in a reign of terror – burning men in the church and pushing women and children over the edge of the sea-cliffs. Donal Cam spent the rest of 1602 in guerrilla activity from the glens of Cork and Kerry, attacking the English troops where he could. He was conscious that sporadic attacks, although satisfactory, were having no significant effect on Carew's forces.

When it became clear towards the end of 1602 that the dilatory Philip III (1578-1621) had lost interest in future involvement in Irish affairs, Donal Cam, partly because of this frustration and a sense that he could no longer depend on his extended family after the treachery of his cousin Owen, began one of the greatest epic journeys in the whole of Irish history. On 31 December 1602 he gathered a train of 1000 followers, 400 of them trusted soldiers and the rest women, children and camp-followers, in Glengarriff, eighteen miles east of Dunboy on Bantry Bay, and headed north for the safety of Ulster, hoping to join O'Neill's army at Lough Neagh. After indescribable hardships, including attacks from local tribes and English forces and in appalling weather, through lands rendered sterile by the 'scorched earth' policies of both Irish and English, he reached the safety of Leitrim Castle, with only thirty-five in his party. Most of the rest had succumbed to illness, hunger, exposure and attack, although some of the soldiers had deserted in order to take up arms with other Irish leaders.

When it seemed that O'Neill had given in to pressure and accepted the terms of the Mellifont agreement, which gave him back all his territories, confirmed him as the Ó Catháin, Lord of the land between the Foyle and the Bann and required an oath of loyalty to James I (1566-1625), Donal Cam could not agree. He hoped for a pardon in 1603 when James VI of Scotland became James I of England but it never came. He left for Spain with his wife and children and accepted a knighthood of the order of St Iago from Philip III, who also created him Earl of Bearhaven. He died in an accidental stabbing, having intervened in a fracas in Madrid. The man who wielded the knife was an Anglo-Irish refugee called John Bathe. Donal Cann's nephew, Philip O'Sullivan Beare, born in the same part of County Cork some time in the 1590s, became famous as the Counter-Reformation historian author of *Historiae Catholiciae Iberniae Compendium* (1621) – a history that, not unexpectedly, gives a lot of space to his uncle's defence of Dunboy and his epic journey.

THE CONFEDERATE WARS 1642-9

BENBURB
6 JUNE 1646

The Battle of Benburb was the only significant success for the Irish side in the Confederate Wars that lasted from 1642 to 1649. The war took its name from the Confederation of Kilkenny, an alliance between Old Irish, Old English and some Catholic New English, formed on 7 June 1642. It was a consequence of the Ulster Rebellion of 1641, a revolt of Catholics dispossessed by the Plantation of Ulster earlier in the century, and Catholic fear of an English parliament that had become increasingly Puritan-dominated. The Old English were loyal to Charles I (1600-49) and the Confederation also included representatives of European powers, notably Giovanni Battista Rinuccini (1592-1663), Archbishop of Fermo and legate of Pope Innocent X (1574-1655).

The Ulster army of the Catholic Confederation was led by Eoghan Rua Ó Néill (1582-49), a nephew of the great Hugh O'Neill, Earl of Tyrone (c. 1550-1616), who had served in European armies since the age of sixteen. A virtual deserter from the army of Spain, he had more than forty years experience of 'modern' warfare and should have been made supreme military commander of the witches' brew that was the Confederation. Robert Monro (d. 1680?), Ó Néill's adversary in the Battle of Benburb, had come from Scotland to defend the Ulster planters from a repetition of the massacres of 1641 and had joined up with local regiments with the intention of attacking the Confederation headquarters in Kilkenny. Although intelligence was slow in communication it was sound enough. Monro knew that Ó Néill was marching north from Glaslough in County Monaghan but, relying on the Irishman's reputation for avoiding confrontation, decided to engage on hillocks at Drumflugh just west of the village of Benburb on the banks of the River Blackwater. Here the river flows due east before turning north into Lough Neagh. The terrain is typical drumlin country, as Monro's army found when it approached from the west over Thistle Hill, having forded the tributary River Oona. There were steep bluffs some 120 feet high and the river hemmed on both sides.

Ó Néill's army was well equipped: with Rinuccini's support and financial aid he was able to muster a significant force of 5000, well supplied with pikes, *sceana* (long knives) and flintlock muskets. He had time to train his men in their use and by June 1646 they were a formidable and, unusually for the Irish, a disciplined fighting force. Monro's tripartite army outnumbered them by a thousand and they had five pieces of artillery, the ultimate weapon of the period, which had been dragged by Monro's men all the way from Poyntz Pass, sixteen crow-fly miles, since the Irish horses were too small. This forced march may have taken the edge off Monro's soldiers since it was made through utterly devastated land with poor roads and evidence all about of the scorched earth policy pursued by both sides. When they reached Benburb the armies in their rather formal way took up their positions close to the river, Ó Néill's forces on a slight rise. The action began when Monro ordered a salvo of his artillery that did not seem to have much effect. A charge of Scots cavalry failed to break the musket and pike wall of the Irish, who were then ordered to advance. The pikemen had no trouble in pushing Monro's men back towards the river. Their formation collapsed after Ó Néill's musketeers fired at point-blank range. Munro's soldiers fled, pursued by the now confident Irish troops, many killed by blade and ball, others drowning in the river. Some were found dead with no sign of injury, apparently from exhaustion.

Between 2000 and 3000 of Munro's forces died in the rout that followed, while Ó Néill's losses were less than 300. It was a mighty victory, with much plundering of the dead and the capture of cannon, muskets and armour. The north was at Ó Néill's mercy. If he had managed to retain his army's full strength (many went home with the spoils) and marched against Derry and Carrickfergus, Charles I might have found in Ireland the support he needed and some kind of recompense might have been made to the dispossessed of Ulster. Further, the lightning Irish campaign of Oliver Cromwell (1599-1658) might have been significantly different. Ó Néill, however, was very much in agreement with Rinuccini's ambition to establish an independent Catholic Ireland, perhaps ruled by Charles I, but preferably by Philip IV (1605-65) of Spain, in spite of his intermittent if remorseful debauchery. He did not capitalise on his success but headed south to become embroiled in murky Confederation politics. He joined forces with James Butler, Duke of Ormond (1610-88), the king's man in Ireland: together they could have met Cromwell (1599-1658) on terms of equality. But Ó Néill died at Cloughoughter near Cavan town on 6 October 1649, three years and four months after his great day, almost certainly of tetanus, although many believed he had been poisoned by enemies.

In the century and a half of nationalist eclipse that followed, the belief that O'Neill's death was treacherous grew steadily. It was the subject of one of Thomas Davis's most famous poems, published in the *Nation* on 19 November 1842:

> 'Did they dare, did they dare, to slay Eoghan Rua Ó Néill?'
> Yes they slew with poison him they feared to meet with steel.'

The rumour locally was that an enemy, a woman, somehow managed to smear a toxin on the inside soles of O'Neill's shoes. These he wore to a festivity 'at which he danced vigorously' and died a few days later, having absorbed the poison through the soles of his feet. He was buried at the Franciscan Abbey in Cavan but no headstone marked his grave, in order to prevent violation by his enemies.

DUNGAN'S HILL
8 AUGUST 1647

Even after Eoghan Rua Ó Néill's (1582-1649) great victory at Benburb in 1646, his rival Thomas Preston (1585-1655), later Viscount Tara, was still regarded by the Catholic Confederation as their chief of men. This was before Preston was excommunicated by the relentless Giovanni Battista Rinuccini (1592-1663), the papal nuncio, for non-compliance. He was given command of the Leinster army, even though, as a garrison commander in Leuven in Belgium and an expert in siege warfare both in defence and attack, he had no experience of the hand-to-hand fighting and deployment of cavalry that would characterise other battles of the Confederate War. That summer Preston's forces were to receive a fiery baptism in aggressive encounters.

As a result of the final defeat and imprisonment of Charles I, the English parliament felt the tactical need to pacify Ireland. Lenient terms were offered to James Butler, 1st Duke of Ormond (1610-88), Butler had earlier had fought the Catholic Confederation as the king's Lord Deputy, but, with a shift of allegiance very characteristic of the war as a whole, he now found himself the de facto ally of the Confederation against the parliamentary New Model Army.

When a large parliamentary army under the command of Colonel Michael Jones arrived in Dublin in June 1647 there was little Ormond could do but accept the terms of surrender offered by Jones. The latter's 4000 foot and 800 horse were very persuasive and by the end of the month Ormond had handed his sword of office to the Roundhead general. Because of this surrender, the city and its immediate surroundings became an anti-royalist enclave. Preston, as chief of the Confederation's eastern army, decided that the Confederates should bring the capital into the Catholic bloc. The chance to do the same for Belfast, then quite a small town and a fief of the Chichesters, had been lost when Ó Néill did not capitalise on his defeat of Monro at Benburb.

The year of 1647 had been one of tedious negotiations and shifting alliances, and it was something of a relief for the Confederation when the Leinster army marched through County Meath in an attempt to emulate Ó Néill's success in Benburb. They hoped to take parliamentary Dublin with a minimum of fuss and casualties but they were intercepted at Dungan's Hill by Roundhead forces. Meath is not known for the height of its hills; Slane and Tara are famous for their historical associations rather than their elevations. Dungan's Hill – its modern location is Summerhill on the road between Maynooth and Trim – would scarcely have been regarded as a hill in, say, Donegal or Kerry. Yet even slight elevations can be significant in a pitched battle. Preston's presence in Meath had seemed to threaten the parliamentary garrison at Trim and Jones had marched to its support, leaving Dublin apparently unguarded.

Preston made a forced march to the Liffey valley, forgetting that infantry marches very slowly, at the speed of the slowest ammunition cart, often to the impatience of the cavalry.

The Confederation army had travelled only twelve of the necessary forty miles when Jones's forces appeared. They occupied the eponymous hill, seized the initiative and forced Preston to position his cavalry in a wooded culvert where they were caught in crossfire. It had been a good summer and now in August the oat and wheat crops were ready for harvesting. Preston's main infantry force was drawn up in the middle of fully ripe wheat, where some of the stalks were more than seven feet tall. The result was that sightlines were occluded and the cavalry was forced to gallop off to regroup. The infantry had been trained to withstand any attack but their attacking ability was not up to the level of their defensive capabilities. There was now no cavalry to protect them as they made their measured way forward. Their lack of mobility was aggravated by the fact that their holding position was in a large field surrounded by a stone wall so that it was easy for the 6000 Roundheads, about equal in number to Preston's force, to surround them and pick them off at leisure.

A detachment of Scots Highlanders, fighting on the Irish side and led by Alasdair Mac Colla, managed to break out of the enclosure and make their way into a bog where Jones's cavalry could no follow. By this means Preston and up to 3000 of his army escaped the field. Many of the remaining 3000 were killed, with only the officers spared to be used for exchange or ransom. One of these prisoners from Preston's army was the seventeen-year-old Richard Talbot (1630-91), son of a local aristocrat, later the rakish Earl of Tyrconnell and Lord Deputy of Ireland for James II (1633-1701) on his accession to the throne in 1685. Those of Preston's army who had escaped were still in danger from Jones's cavalry, who were in hot pursuit, but Eoghan Rua Ó Néill, having heard of the catastrophe, arrived in time to challenge them. When Jones became aware that the victorious army of Benburb was in the vicinity, he headed back to Dublin. It was a humiliating defeat for the Confederation and greatly weakened its future ability to engage with Oliver Cromwell (1599-1658). It also widened the split between the Royalist and Irish parties in Kilkenny.

Knocknanoss
13 November 1647

Of the players in the long-drawn-out drama of the Confederate War (1642-53) none is more characteristic than Murrough O'Brien (1614-74), later Lord Inchiquin. During his public career he made other opportunists seem grotesquely incompetent and was a real life Vicar of Bray. He married the daughter of William St Leger, Lord President of Munster, an alliance that required that he relinquish Catholicism, his first religion. He saw military service in Italy in 1639 and on is return was appointed deputy governor of Munster to and by his father-in-law and governor of Munster on St Leger's death. There were in those years essentially two rival systems of government, that of the king and that of Parliament. O'Brien had been frustrated in his bid to be appointed Lord President of Munster by Charles I but with his highly developed sense of self-advancement he realised that the king's rule would not last and that his future lay with parliament.

To this end he established his Protestant credentials during the years 1644-7 by proving himself the chief adversary of the Catholic Confederation in the province. He used his army of 4500 to expel the Catholics of Cork, Youghal and Kinsale and captured the garrisons of Dungarvan and Cappoquin. He was known to the Irish as *Murchadh na dTóiteann* ('Murrough the Burner') because of his ruthlessness in setting fire to farms and destroying crops to prevent the Confederates from living off the land, in his tergiversations in religion, loyalties and tactics, he was a kind of metaphor for the unholy *mélange* that was the Catholic

Confederation. Mostly on the side of the parliament, he was often content to fight against it if he had reason.

In the late autumn of 1647 Murrough O'Brien was responsible for inflicting the second crippling defeat on the Confederation in three months, annihilating the army of Munster in Knocknanuss, County Cork, as successfully as Jones had that of Leinster at Dungan's Hill in County Meath. O'Brien's preparations for the battle were meticulous and ruthless. All through the summer of 1647 he had applied his usual 'scorched earth' policy throughout the rich fields of Munster, justly earning his nickname. Because of internecine and endemic in-fighting, the Confederation of Kilkenny could not mount any army capable of opposing him, although he was clearly the enemy of both the native Irish and the Royalists. When O'Brien assaulted the iconic Rock of Cashel, piled burning peat against its wooden palisade and massacred the garrison and the unarmed priests, the Confederation's supreme council was at last stirred into action. They dismissed Donagh MacCarthy, Viscount Muskerry, the Munster general, replacing him with Theobald Taafe, Ist Earl of Carlingford, an English Catholic, with little battle experience. He had with him the veteran Highland chief Alasdair MacColla, whose Scots troops had fought so bravely at Dungan's Hill in the summer. Taafe's dilettantism was demonstrated by his suggestion to his adversary that the battle should be fought by 2000 foot-soldiers 'more for recreation than for any serious purpose'. O'Brien kept his face straight when he rejected the suggestion. He had more than 5000 troops and he planned to engage a Confederation army two thousand greater in numbers. His troops were well-trained and rich with the plunder of the summer depredations. Most were professional soldiers, who had been imported from England, bolstered by a large contingent of Scots and English planters from Ulster, eager to seek for revenge for the plantation massacres of 1641.

Taafe's army was taken by surprise by O'Brien at Knocknanuss – *Cnoc na nOs* ('Deerhill') – a hill about 500 feet high three miles east of Kanturk, in MacCarthy's country in County Cork. For some inexplicable reason, Taafe positioned his men on opposite sides of the hill so that communication between the two wings was impossible. Mac Colla's men attacked the parliamentary forces opposite them, killing many and putting the rest to flight. Assuming that the battle was over, they picked up what spoils were available from the abandoned baggage train. But on the other side of the hill, O'Brien's seasoned cavalry routed the inexperienced Irishmen, sending them flying down the slope. Once deprived of their horsemen the Irish infantry ran away, abandoning equipment and weapons. Mac Colla's men surrendered, expecting honourable treatment, but they were simply slaughtered on O'Brien's instructions. Few Irishmen were spared; even the day after the battle, a party of Irish soldiers found sheltering in a copse were summarily executed. The total death toll on the Irish side was in excess of 3000, the 1000 dead Parliamentarians mainly dispatched by Mac Colla's Highlanders.

Dungan's Hill and Knocknanuss between them finished the Catholic cause. There was nothing left for the Confederates but to make what peace they could with the Royalists and await the result of the Roundheads' victory in the English Civil War and the coming of Oliver Cromwell (1599-1658). Among O'Brien's officers was George Monck (1608-70), later Duke of Albemarle, who afterwards was the chief agent in the restoration to the British throne of Charles II (1630-85). O'Brien, with enviable elasticity, joined the Confederation and, when Cromwell and his successors caused it to disappear in fire and exile after 1649, he left for France to become a valued member of the court in exile of Charles II. Charles, always generous to his brothers in exile, rewarded him in 1654 with the title of 1st Earl of Inchiquin. Murrough died, a Catholic again, in 1674, having lived quietly at Rostellan in Cork harbour for the final ten years of his life.

Rathmines
20 August 1649

During what one can loosely term the Confederate Wars, when dissension between anti-parliamentary allies spoiled chance after chance of victory, a total of thirty-three battles was fought. Only one, the Battle of Benburb, engineered by the brilliant Eoghan Rua Ó Néill (1582-1649), was a decisive victory for the Catholic Confederation. If Eoghan Rua had been given supreme command instead of Thomas Preston and if he had not died prematurely, many believed by treachery, the history of seventeenth-century Ireland might have been significantly different.

After the defeats at Dungan's Hill and Knocknanuss, the Catholics had no option but to come to terms with Charles I's Royalist forces led by James Butler, 1st Duke of Ormond (1610-88). An army of Irish Catholics and 'Old English' Catholics led by Ormond attempted to oust Colonel Michael Jones, the Parliamentary commander in Dublin: an affray that became known at the battle of Rathmines. This was typically ironic of the Ireland of the time in that it was Ormond who had relinquished Dublin to Jones two years earlier. Jones had been the victor at Dungan's Hill and had a great reputation as a lively and aggressive commander; his holding of Dublin was as much symbolic as tactical. Indeed any Confederation victory was merely temporising: since the execution of the king on 31 January 1649 it was only a matter of time until Cromwell (1599-1658), the victor of the two civil wars in Britain, should arrive to avenge the slaughter of the Ulster colonists eight years before. It was as much to please the outlawed Charles II (1630-85), whom he soon joined in exile, as for any Catholic advantage, that Ormond was carrying on the fight.

Ormond marshalled an army of 11,000 and, approaching the capital from the south, captured Rathfarnham Castle. He set up his main camp at what is now Palmerston Park in Rathgar with outposts in Ranelagh and Rathgar. In those years the city ended at St Stephen's Green. An extra urgency was given by the news that Cromwell was about to embark for Ireland. Ormond sent Colonel Purcell with 1500 men to occupy the ruinous Baggotsrath Castle (sited at today's Baggot Street Bridge) that would cover the Dodder and Ringsend. Purcell was a stranger to the region and was given wrong instructions. It was dawn on 2 August before he was able to occupy the old fort and almost immediately he was attacked by a surprise force of Jones's cavalry from the north-west. The survivors fled south and west to Ranelagh. Ormond was a careful slow-moving commander and was taken totally by surprise by Jones's move. There was understandable confusion in Ormond's camp as he hurriedly drew up defensive lines against Jones's centre.

Jones's cavalry had swung right round behind Ormond's army and had begun to attack from the rear. Even though Jones had less than half the strength of Ormond his men could move much more rapidly: his foot soldiers routed the Confederate soldiers and his horse harried them as they fled. The death toll would have been much greater had not Murrough O'Brien (1614-74), the victor of Knocknanuss, now fighting alongside his old Catholic enemies, organised his English Royalist army into a rearguard action that held off Jones's main thrust, allowing many of Ormond's Irish troops to escape.

There were the usual claims and counter-claims, Ormond insisting that his losses were fewer than 1000 and Jones claiming that the figure was nearer 3000, with 2500 prisoners. Jones's continued control of Dublin allowed Cromwell to land at Ringsend with 15,000 seasoned troops ready for the reconquest of

Ireland. With his customary assurance and quasi-mystic language Cromwell described Rathmines as 'an astonishing mercy, so great and seasonable that we are like them that dreamed' and set to with gusto to continue the Almighty's work. Jones who had proved several times to be a doughty commander, could be excused for exclaiming: 'Never was any day in Ireland like this...'

Before Rathmines the Royalist/Catholic alliance controlled most of Ireland, except for Derry and Dublin: the taking of Dublin was regarded as a matter of form. Things changed utterly after that. Throughout the Byzantine complications of the Confederate Wars, the Irish advantage was continually vitiated by the incompetence in its generals – with the notable exception of Eoghan Ó Néill, whose death later in 1649 put paid to any Irish hope of withstanding Cromwell. Ormond eventually went to France and joined Charles II, whom he had proclaimed king on his father's execution. The battle of Rathmines has continued to fascinate Dubliners, especially as the city grew to cover with streets and houses the various sites of the battle. It is said that the well-known Dublin pub, 'The Bleeding Horse', on a corner in Upper Camden Street, owes its name to a wounded cavalry mount that wandered into an inn at that point, and for many years afterwards the scene of the fighting round Rathgar was known as the 'Bloody Fields'.

An element of Confederation intrigue could not be kept out of this straightforward struggle between Royalist and Roundhead. The Machiavellian hand of Giovanni Battista Rinuccini (1592-1663), Archbishop of Fermo and legate of Pope Innocent (1574-1655), the most vigorous promoter of the Counter-Reformation in Ireland, could not bear to support any Catholic/Royalist alliance that was not under his control. It is likely that under the archbishop's instructions his agent Edmond O'Reilly (1598-1669), Archbishop of Armagh, arranged for Ormond's men to be led astray by their guide.

CROMWELL'S WAR 1649-50

DROGHEDA
11 SEPTEMBER 1649

Oliver Cromwell (1599-1658) landed in Ireland on 15 August 1649, determined to put down Royalist disaffection and perhaps unaware of his visceral need to avenge the overstated massacres of Ulster planters in 1641. The skilful New Model Army tactician almost immediately turned his attention to Drogheda, 'one of the best fortified towns in Ireland'. It looked both north and south, and was essentially an Old English town loyal to the recently executed Charles I (1600-49) and his son Charles II (1630-85), the king in exile. The need to extirpate any Royalist support was even more important to Cromwell than to avenge the Ulster killings. The one-legged commander of Drogheda, Sir Arthur Aston, may have irritated him with his schoolboy claim that anyone who could take Drogheda 'could capture Hell itself'. The answer to the boast was that it might be vulnerable to the devil himself.

The River Boyne is navigable at least as far as the town of Drogheda and it was a simple matter for Sir George Ayscue to bring his parliamentarian fleet right to the walls and have two artillery batteries set up on the south bank. One was aimed at the southern wall between the Duleek Gate and St Mary's Church, where the church tower was used as a lookout post by Aston. The other cannon was aimed at the wall to the east. Also on the south bank was the prehistoric Millmount, fortified by ditch, bank and palisade.

Cromwell organised his men into five regiments, commanded by colonels Castle and Ewer, who attacked from the south,

Hewson, on the east, and Venables and Phayre who acted as second-line support.

On 10 September Cromwell called upon Aston to surrender and upon receiving the refusal ordered the barrage to begin. By noon on the following day two breaches had been made in the south and east walls, wide enough to permit the Parliamentarian troops to enter the town. Resistance was fierce on both flanks. The eastern attack was repulsed and Hewson's troops began to retreat down the steep cliff they had just scaled. Support came from Venables and Phayre and a strong force was then able to surged into the centre of the town. The southern attack wavered when Colonel Castle was killed by a bullet to the head. An almost certain retreat was prevented only by Cromwell's charging into the breach and rallying the faltering insurgents. The death of Colonel Wall, the Royalist commander, totally unnerved the defenders and Cromwell's troops occupied the parts of the town north of the river.

Aston and about three hundred of his troops fell back to try to hold the Millmount but the wooden defences were easily broken down. In a messianic mood, Cromwell ordered that no quarter be given. All were killed: Aston was savagely beaten to death with his own wooden leg that the parliamentary army believed was filled with gold sovereigns. The Cromwellians charged through the town, killing officers and men, and even priests and monks whom they affected to believe were combatants. A number of townsfolk took refuge in St Peter's Church and were burned alive when Cromwell set fire to the building. Of many actions that caused the name of Cromwell to be execrated throughout Ireland, the massacre at Drogheda was the most heinous.

WEXFORD
2-11 OCTOBER 1649

Wexford was also a target for Oliver Cromwell (1599-1658), partly because of the expulsion of Protestants from the town in 1642 by Lord Mountgarret, the local Confederate commander during the Confederate Wars. Eighty of them had died in an accidental drowning in a boat that was taking them away from Wexford and this was conflated in Cromwell's mind with the other anti-Protestant horrors of 1641. Wexford, too, was the home of Confederate privateers, who were the scourge of local shipping – especially those of the parliament – in the Irish Sea. At least forty of these near-pirates operated from the south-eastern port, tolerated by the Confederate ruler in Kilkenny because of the ten per cent of their booty that was delivered to them. The town has an extensive, almost landlocked harbour where the River Slaney widens out and contracts again at Rosslare Point. It was one of the strongholds of the Confederate/Royalist axis and as such, like Drogheda, a prime target for the Parliamentary army.

Cromwell arrived at the town on 2 October 1649 with 6000 troops of his 'invincible' New Model Army. Admiral Deane, the commander of the English navy, was able to bring his ships into Wexford Harbour because the undermanned fort at Rosslare Point had made no attempt to hinder him. Eight siege guns and two mortars were set upon a rise south of the town and were ready for firing on 6 October. On 3 October Cromwell's formal demand that the town surrender was received by David Sinnott, the Irish commander. Foul weather allowed Sinnott to play for time and build up his troops from 1500 to an approximate 5000 by 11 October, the extra soldiers arriving at the north end of the port. Sinnott temporised because he was aware that disease was rife among Cromwell's men . Although they had plenty of arms, rations were scarce. He knew, too, that the main Royalist/ Confederate army under the Duke of Ormond (1610-88) was only a score of miles away at New Ross. His answer to Cromwell made what in the circumstances were extremely arrogant conditions. He demanded free practice of the Catholic religion, free evacuation of the armed defenders and licence for the privateer fleet to find another safe haven.

The Protector's response was to blow two holes in the walls of Wexford Castle, leaving the town extremely vulnerable. The negotiations came to a sudden end, probably without Cromwell's instruction. A letter from him to Sinnott on 11 October agreed to some of the conditions and promised that the troops would have quarter and that the ordinary inhabitants of the town and their property would be secure. In the middle of these negotiations, after the inexplicable surrender by the English Royalist commander of the castle, Cromwell's troops attacked. The result was a rerun of Drogheda with wholesale slaughter of troops, clergy and 1500 civilians The ones who were not shot or put to the sword were drowned trying to swim across the Slaney. The town was looted and then set on fire. Cromwell's involvement in the slaughter has been a matter for debate with historians since. Cromwell insisted that he did not order the sack of the town but vigorously defended the actions of his men. Another crime had been added to the list of his villainies.

CLONMEL
17 MAY 1650

By the spring of 1650 Cromwell's Irish campaign was running out of steam. His 'invincible' New Model Army was decimated by plague and by the attrition caused by taking such Royalist/ Confederate towns as Dundalk, Drogheda and Wexford. Increasing demands from London that he return to face a new Royalist threat from Scotland meant that he had to prepare to leave Ireland, as he did on 26 May. However, he had his eye on Clonmel as a last prize before leaving his son-in-law Henry Ireton (1611-51) to continue the terror initiated by and usually accredited to his father-in-law. The town occupies the north bank of the River Suir, twenty-five miles from the still unconquered Waterford. Its northern, western and eastern sides were well defended by walls six feet thick and twenty feet high. These were further strengthened by earthworks with a deep ditch behind them. The river was the town's main defence on the southern side.

The other advantage the defenders had was their commander, Hugh Dubh O'Neill (d.1660), a nephew of Eoghan Rua Ó Néill (1582-49). Like his uncle he was a seasoned campaigner, a high-ranker in the army of Spain and, finally insignificant as it was, he managed to inflict a considerable defeat on Cromwell. Parliamentary forces had maintained a loose blockade round the town since the previous February and food and armaments were scarce inside the town. O'Neill believed that the Duke of Ormond (1610-88) with the main anti-parliamentary army was on its way from Ulster. His purpose was to hold out in Clonmel for as long as possible so that Cromwell would at last be faced with an army that could meet him on roughly equal terms.

Cromwell arrived at the scene on 27 April with an 8000 infantry, 600 cavalry and twelve field guns. Clearly his intention was to take the town in a kind of Blitzkrieg rather than use the tactic of a long siege and starvation. Cromwell needed heavier artillery to breach the walls and when this artillery arrived it was discovered that it could not be set up except on the northern side. There were marshes to the east and west of the town and the River Suir to the south. O'Neill had calculated on breaches in the northern walls and had built a V-shaped corridor that seemed to lead into the heart of the town but was in reality a (literal) dead end. The sides of the corridor had been built up with earth and wood to a height of six feet and behind it O'Neill placed his best marksmen with muskets on both sides and what small cannon he possessed at the apex of the angle. The English soldiers had no difficulty in storming through the breach and advancing along O'Neill's corridor. They were raked by musket-fire and chain shot from the cannon but were unable to retreat because of the surge of fresh soldiers coming in. At least 1000 foot soldiers were killed before the rest fought their way back out.

Urged by their general to make another assault, the infantry refused to attempt a second charge and even the steely Cromwell assented. His cavalrymen had helmets and body armour and the commanders volunteered to lead them dismounted as heavily armoured infantry. The use of horses in such a situation would have been lunacy and not even the most tunnel-visioned captains favoured it. At their approach the Irish defenders slipped deeper into the wedge and turned to face the Cromwellian forces in a bloody hand-to-hand battle that lasted three hours. The armour in which the English trusted proved more handicap than advantage and the cavalry too were forced to retreat. Cromwell lost between 1500 and 2500 men, including some of his best officers and did not dare attempt to take Clonmel again. The alternative, which would probably have worked eventually, was a long siege. He was anxious to attend to the more pressing business of Charles II's advance from Scotland with his Presbyterian army.

It was the most serious repulse the 'invincible' army had sustained but O'Neill was in no position to capitalise upon his success: he had lost several hundred men and exhausted his stores of ammunition. The townspeople were starving and he had no food to feed his soldiers. There was no sign of the help much promised by Ormond. O'Neill decided that evacuation was the only alternative. The night after the withdrawal of the New Model Army he sent his army in small groups across the Suir to the south bank where there were no English troops with the instruction that they make for Waterford. The relentless Cromwell sent his cavalry after them as soon as he learned of the abandonment of the town. He was able to dispatch only a few stragglers: the majority safely reached Waterford. Thomas Preston (1585-1655), Eoghan Rua Ó Néill's main Confederate rival, proved uncooperative as ever with the Ulstermen and refused them refuge. O'Neill had no alternative but to help them make their way back north. A year later, as governor of Limerick, he was forced to surrender the city to Ireton and was condemned to death. His sentenced was commuted and he was later released on exile to Spain, where he died in 1660.

Scarriffhollis
21 June 1650

The death of Eoghan Rua Ó Néill on 6 November 1649 was a grievous blow to the Catholic Confederation, even though not all grieved. His support of the Counter-Reformation policy of Giovanni Battista Rinuccini (1592-1663), Archbishop of Fermo and legate of Pope Innocent X (1574-1655), had alienated the Royalist faction. By numbers alone the Catholic lobby were able to outvote the rest of the supreme council of the Confederation and it was almost inevitable that the papal legate would have the main say in choosing Ó Néill's successor.

The aristocracy and clergy of Ulster met at Belturbet on 18 May 1650 and considered several candidates, including the Marquis of Antrim, the leader most likely to reconcile the Ulster Scots and the northern Catholics growing daily more fearful at the news from the south. The clergy were easily able to insist that their candidate should become commander in spite of all the rhetoric and lobbying of Ormond, the leader of the Royalist party in Ireland. For this reason the choice of Heber MacMahon (1600-50), late Bishop of Down and Connor and now Bishop of Clogher, was political rather than practical. He had no military experience but his support for Rinuccini and the Counter-Reformation was impeccable, and neither Taafe nor Preston, the Munster and Leinster commanders, had done well in the field. Ormond was on the point of leaving to join Charles II in his French exile but was persuaded, strongly against his instincts, to sign MacMahon's commission, on 1 April 1650.

It seemed to MacMahon that his first task was to create a diversion in Ulster to take some of the heat from the Cromwellian ravaging in the east and south. By late May 1650 he had gathered together an army of 4000 infantry and 600 cavalry at Loughgall, five miles from Charlemont in County Armagh. The chief Cromwellian commander in Ulster was Sir Charles Coote (d.1661) but because his troops were stationed at different garrisons about the province the largest force he could muster against MacMahon was 800 foot and 600 horsemen. The bishop moved north through the Sperrins and took Dungiven in County Derry. According to the custom of the time the garrison of Protestants were all killed except for the commander who was sent as a hostage to Charlemont. The capture of Coleraine and Ballycastle followed without much difficulty. Lacking a supply base so far from any Confederation stronghold, MacMahon decided to drive westward and face Coote before his adjutant Colonel Venables could come to his aid.

Coote's army was encamped at Lifford, County Donegal, fifteen miles south of Derry, and MacMahon reached there on 2 June. After four hours MacMahon seemed to withdraw across the Deele River. Coote sent his cavalry to attack the rearguard but it was driven back by the Irish cavalry. It was then that MacMahon's lack of tactical experience proved disastrous. It would have been the perfect time to attack Coote. Instead he ordered the army north-west and it encamped on a hillside at Scarriffhollis, on the banks of the River Swilly, three miles from Letterkenny, to await Coote.

By now the Coote's army had been strengthened by Venables' force and it reached Scarriffhollis by 21 June. The defensive position was good and MacMahon's troops still outnumbered the combined Cromwellian forces. He was in a pugnacious mood and berated his wiser officers – including Sir Phelim O'Neill (c. 1604-53), for their suggestion that they hold their positions. He arranged his forces in a solid bloc with musketeers in front, formidable to the enemy but leaving little room for manoeuvre.

Coote preferred smaller groups, rather like raiding parties, ready to withdraw on command. A Colonel Fenwick led the first sortie of 150 Roundheads and although he was killed in the attack the formation of the Irish vanguard began to weaken and fall back. They continued to fight with musket-butts and pikes but as they retreated they could not break the solid formation of their own infantry. This hampered their capacity to retaliate by depriving them of room to manoeuvre. The English musketeers, unhurried and with time and space to reload, poured a steady stream of fire on the crowded Irish, inflicting heavy damage. A flank attack by Coote caused further severe casualties and the Irish began to run away. It was a complete rout, with Coote's cavalry pursuing the Irish infantry for ten miles to Breenagh and beyond. The Protestant settlers joined vigorously in the pursuit, again in revenge for 1641. Coote ordered the execution of all prisoners and hanged the wounded MacMahon at Enniskillen on 12 September. Three thousand Irish soldiers were killed in the battle, while the English toll was only three hundred.

The battle of Scarriffhollis meant the end of significant resistance to the English parliamentary armies. Charlemont Fort, commanded by Sir Phelim O'Neill – who had managed to escape from Scarriffhollis by hard riding – held out until 14 August, in spite of heavy artillery attacks. O'Neill surrendered on terms that, unusually, were honoured. He fled to a refuge in County Tyrone where he survived until 1653, when he was betrayed by a kinsman. He was executed on 10 March.

THE WAR OF THE THREE KINGS 1688-91

THE SIEGE OF DERRY
7 DECEMBER 1688-1 AUGUST 1689

The Williamite war, known to Irish contemporaries as *Cogadh an Dá Rí*, was from a European viewpoint part the War of the *Three* Kings, as Spain, Britain, Holland, Austria, Bavaria and even the pope combined to stay the ungovernable territorial ambitions of Louis XIV of France (1638-1715). Even the relinquishing of the English throne by James II (1633-1701) although of consuming interest to these islands, was of little more than conversational significance in Europe. He was still legally King of Ireland and it was from that country that he hoped to recover his power.

James's first move after landing in Dublin and setting up a partially new regime was to move towards the 'maiden city' to demand allegiance. This seemed to be flouted when the thirteen orphan apprentices closed the Ferryquay Gate at the south-east end of the walled city against the Catholic Earl of Antrim's Redshanks (as the kilted mercenaries were called). They had arrived from Limavady and crossed from the east bank by ferry on 7 December 1688 to stand down the Protestant garrison. The other three gates were soon closed and the famous siege had begun.

The gates were soon opened again and the siege did not reach a serious level of military blockade, with a boom across the River Foyle to prevent any succour by water, until the public humiliation of the king at the south-west Bishop's Gate. He stood for hours in the spring rain on 18 April 1689, having ridden in from his bivouac at Raphoe to arrive at the nearest gate. Colonel

Robert Lundy (d. 1717), the city's governor, advised surrender and has by that perfectly loyal and logical advice earned perennial execration with Ulster Protestants, who made the name Lundy into a common noun meaning 'traitor'. It was on that morning that the iconic words, 'No surrender,' were hurled at the king, accompanied by a discharge of musketry and cannonballs that killed several of the royal party, including Captain Troy, one of the king's aide-de-camps.

The besieged had certain advantages: they outnumbered the besiegers and had greater firepower. The walls were impregnable and the motley collection of Irish-speaking, English and French soldiers were without shelter in the continuous summer rain. There was no acceptable commander-in-chief and Rosen, the Lithuanian commander of the French, urged a policy of frightfulness when he arrived on 20 June. His sound military instinct was to blast the city into surrender but he was reluctantly dissuaded because the toll of civilian casualties would have been intolerable, even by the standards of the time. It was the obvious tactic since the little hilly city was surrounded by much higher hills and had no cannon except for those few trained on the lough against possible relief forces. Rosen's next suggestion was to round up all the Protestants from the surrounding districts (1200 people in all) and hang them one after the other outside the city gates until the defenders yielded or permitted the hostages to enter the beleaguered city and further deplete their scant rations. Again he was dissuaded, reminded by Richard Hamilton, the chief English officer, that the king had commanded that unarmed Protestants should be left unharmed.

There were a few fierce skirmishes: at Pennyburn, north of the city, on 21 April, at an old windmill to the south on 5 May and at Butcher Gate, the north-west access, on 21 June. The final tactical decision because of the level of desertion and disease among the besiegers was to starve the inhabitants into submission. According to firmly believed myth the original population of 2000 was inflated by 30,000 Protestant refugees and 7000 soldiers; and they are said to have been forced to eat mice, rats and dogs that had originally fed on unburied corpses. In fact the total population that could have physically crowded into the walled section and an approximately equal area of outer defences to the south was about 10,000, and the fatalities, mainly women and children, would have been at most 5000 and not the usual propagandist figure of 15,000.

What made the plight of the besieged so heartbreaking was the sight four miles downstream of a Williamite relief fleet unable to reach the city because of a boom, made of timber and cables to the design of the Marquis de Pointis, the French head of artillery, stretched across the sandbanks where the River Foyle meets the lough. The Williamite Major-General Percy Kirke was initially reluctant to have his ships risk the continual barrage of artillery at the boom but in desperation made a successful feint, getting *Dartmouth* to engage the Jacobite cannon while the sailors in a longboat from the *Swallow* sufficiently weakened the boom to allow the transports *Mountjoy* and *Phoenix* to crash through. Three days later, on 1 August, the motley armies of James II limped away. It was an unpropitious start to his campaign.

For all its comparative insignificance the siege has passed into Protestant iconography and is celebrated twice yearly by the Apprentice Boys of Derry, an order similar to the Orange Order but wearing Derry-crimson sashes. A giant effigy of the 'traitor' Lundy, packed full of fireworks, is burned around 18 December (the anniversary, new style since the Gregorian calendar had finally been accepted) of the shutting of the Ferryquay Gate and there is a march including a circuit of the walls on 12 August, to celebrate the 'Relief of Derry'.

NEWTOWNBUTLER
31 JULY 1689

The traditional Orange song, 'The Sash My Father Wore' has for the second line of its first verse: 'It was worn at Derry, Aughrim, Enniskillen and the Boyne.' It fits well with the rhyme and rhythm of the song but the order is not chronological and there was no actual battle of Enniskillen. Townspeople of Enniskillen did, however, take part in the conflict on the side of William III (1650-1702). They ignored an order by Robert Lundy (d. 1717), Protestant but loyal to James II, the governor of the siege city until the beginning of the siege, to report to Derry and align themselves with the inhabitants, instead setting themselves up as a guerrilla force with the town as base. Their targets were Jacobite villages like Trillick, Augher and Clones in Tyrone, Fermanagh and Monaghan.

Such was the reputation of the 'Inniskilliniers', who were of the same temper as the besieged of Derry, that the multinational Jacobite army besieging the city dreaded an attack from them. They were coming to the unsuccessful end of the siege in the summer of 1689 and believed that they had more to fear from them than the Derry Williamites. They had become so much of a nuisance that an army of 3000 under the command of Justin McCarthy, Viscount Mountcashel, was sent to quell them. Most of the soldiers of McCarthy's army were inexperienced, mainly conscripts recruited from the families on his estates. McCarthy's army had some cannon and when on 28 July 1689 they camped at Newtownbutler, twenty miles from Enniskillen, they found themselves close enough to Crom Castle on Upper Lough Erne to bombard then they retreated to their camp. Two days later a party of Jacobite dragoons was ambushed at Lisnaskea, six miles north of Crom on the road to Enniskillen, and 230 men were killed. The rest would have been taken prisoner had not McCarthy arraigned his main force against the ambush party, who was under the command of Colonel Berry.

William Wolesley, the chief of the 'Inniskilliniers', now came from the town with about 2000 soldiers and met Mountcashel's men a mile south of Newtownbutler. Even though the Jacobites outnumbered the Williamites by at least 1000, the difference in number was not significant for most of the untried Jacobite troops ran away when the shooting began. They were hunted down by Williamite cavalry led by Lieutenant-Colonel Tiffin, who cut to pieces 1500 of them and drove 500 into Upper Lough Erne. Only one man succeeded in swimming to safety. Four hundred Jacobite officers were captured and exchanged for Williamite prisoners. These included Mountcashel, who was badly wounded but lived to command the Irish Brigade in France. He survived by sheer good luck: as he lay on the field an Inniskillinier was about to club him to death when a Jacobite prisoner identified him as their general.

The successes of Wolseley and Tiffin included mopping-up operations on stragglers from Derry once the siege was over. The result was that the Jacobite forces in Ulster were weakened and the landing of the Williamite Duke of Schomberg with 20,000 men at Bangor in County Down was unopposed. In a sense Newtownhamilton was a bloody prelude to the less bloody clash at the Boyne.

THE BOYNE
1 JULY 1690

The Boyne is nominally one of the best-known battles in Irish history, although its chief celebrators are not too precise about its actual details. It was enough that King Billy, the affectionate name for William III (1650-1702), beat James II (1633-1701), *Séamas an Chaca* ('James the Shit'), so named by his disappointed Irish supporters, after his perceived dereliction during the battle. William too is seen on many Orange banners and decorative arches showing his valour in crossing the river on a white horse. It was not the decisive battle of *Cogadh an Dá Rí* (The War of the Two Kings) – it was merely a sideshow in the wars against Louis XIV (1636-1701) – but it was the one that eventually gave the Orange Order its yearly celebration. The simplification of ignorance lasts longer than boring old facts: that King Billy's horse was sorrel, which provided its name; that he was tolerant of Catholics, opposed the Popery Laws and had many Dutch Catholics in his army. The New Style calendar Adapted in 1752 meant that the celebration of the anniversary takes place on 'the Twelfth 12 July as around it would come' when many 'played on the flute to the sound of the drum' as one of the few comic Orange songs reminds us.

The battle was fought near the village of Oldbridge on the River Boyne with the village of Slane to the west and the town of Drogheda to the east making convenient markers of the extent of the battlegrounds. It was the first fixed clash in the Protestant mantra- 'Derry, Aughrim, Enniskillen and the Boyne', achronological for euphony, and the only one in which James II took part.

William landed at Carrickfergus on the north shore of Belfast Lough on 14 June 1690 with the intention of taking Dublin, as much for the propaganda value as for any real tactical advantage. When he joined Frederick Herman, Duke of Schomberg (1615-90) they had 30,000 troops in total, consisting of English in whom William had no confidence, his own crack Dutch Blue Guards, some of whom carried the papal flag as Catholics, and Danes commanded by the Duke of Würtemburg-Neustadt who, later in the year, shared with Marlborough the credit for the capture of Cork and Kinsale. James's army had Irish and French regiments with a total muster of 23,000 men. After assembling his men at Loughbrickland, between Banbridge and Newry, William headed south towards Dundalk. (Schomberg had wintered there, having landed at Bangor the previous August with 20,000 troops, but many deserted during the winter while a number died from typhoid and other diseases and Schomberg's army was still ravaged by pestilence. Somewhat illogically William blamed the duke for the condition of his men but he may also have nourished an ageist objection to a seventy-five-year-old commander.)

A section of William's army could have been stopped or at least delayed at the Moyry Pass that had figured in so many Irish battles in the past. Even the main force that marched through Newry could have been hindered, but for some reason James decided to fall back towards the Boyne river that flows from Westmeath in a north-easterly direction until it turns due east at Slane to reach the sea at Drogheda. It has throughout its length, many loops and bends and the one at Oldbridge was to prove severely to James's disadvantage.

Oldbridge was the best place to ford the river between Slane and Drogheda, which was held by the Jacobites. The Blue Guards, having forced their way south across the river, were pinned down by the cavalry, mainly from Irish aristocratic families hoping to recover from the disabilities imposed by Cromwell and not removed by Charles II. It was during this riverside encounter that Schomberg was killed, as was George Walker (c. 1646-90) who had declared himself governor of Derry after Lundy's flight from the city. He had managed to write an account of the famous siege without mentioning that at least a third of the stalwart defenders were Presbyterian. At this point the Williamite forces were in danger of death either from musket fire or by drowning in the Boyne and the battle was going James's way. William sent a quarter of his reserve forces under Count Meinhardt Schomberg, the duke's son, to cross the river at Rosnaree, two miles on the Slane side of Oldbridge, and swing round behind the main Jacobite lines. They were met by 600 dragoons led by Sir Neil O'Neill. These fought well but they had no chance against Schomberg's mixture of 7000 cavalry and foot. In a panic, James diverted two thirds of his troops to help O'Neill, thus severely weakening his ability to stop William's troops in the centre.

James's move proved pointless since a deep gully and a ditch kept the two forces apart. He had brought nearly all his artillery but because of the nature of the terrain was unable to use the guns against Schomberg. Stripped of guns, the Jacobites were unable to hold William's centre attack and fell back towards Duleek. The retreat was orderly because of the fierce rearguard action of the Jacobite cavalry led by Richard Talbot, 1st Earl of Tyrconnell (1630-91), James's viceroy and military second-in-command. This action allowed the retreating army successfully to cross the River Nanny at Duleek, a village four miles due south of Oldbridge and five miles from Drogheda. For such a large gathering of men, about 50,000 in all, the casualty figures were low – about 1500 Jacobites and only 500 Williamites. The Boyne saw little in the way of close fighting and the disposition of artillery meant that deadly blowing to bits by relentless cannonballs was minimal. Most of the deadly wounds were inflicted on an army already conquered and in flight. Tyrconnell's cavalry prevented wholesale slaughter but the greatest damage inflicted was psychological. There were many desertions of Irish soldiers and the remainder abandoned Dublin and fell back towards Limerick.

James's hasty departure weakened the position of his loyal followers at home but they fought on with some help from France. The victory was not only William's; it was the first victory for the partners of the League of Augsburg, who were determined that France should not become the super-power in Europe. It was ironic that the two chief collaborators were Pope Alexander VIII (1610-91) and King Billy – a blasphemous concept to modern Unionists. A *Te Deum* was sung in the Stephansdom in Vienna because James had been defeated. The loss of nerve in James II who was a competent general and a brilliant admiral is hard to fathom. The Jacobite army was more or less intact but James probably had a vision of a long drawn-out war with a steadily diminishing hope of regaining the English throne. That evening in Dublin, so the story goes, James railed at Tyrconnell's wife, 'The Irish have run well!' Her response is now part of the *béaloideas*: 'You, sire, seemed to have beaten them.' Only Frances Jennings (d.1731), Marlborough's sister-in-law, would have had the self-confidence as an unregenerate Catholic to utter it. The Boyne was a significant victory but need not have been the end for Jacobite hopes.

THE FIRST SIEGE OF LIMERICK
7-27AUGUST 1690

In 1690 Limerick was a sizable town built on an island in the estuary of the River Shannon. Its walls were in poor shape; Lauzun, one of the French officers among the defenders, said that roasted apples could breach them, let alone cannonballs, but in spite of this its position made it hard to capture. There were nearly 15,000 Jacobite troops in the city and north of the river in County Clare 2500 cavalry under the command of Patrick Sarsfield (*c.* 1655-93). Although the Jacobite troops who had left the field at the Boyne were in disarray, Sarsfield had sufficient charisma and control over their officers to meld them into a fighting force again.

William III (1650-1702) and his army of 25,000 reached the Shannon on 7 August 1690, a week after his success at the Boyne. He occupied two forts on the south bank of the Shannon, built in the usual pentagonal style in 1650 and named after heroes of the British Commonwealth, Ireton and Cromwell, but was unable to make much impression on the town with only light field artillery.

An expected siege train with the necessary heavy cannon was on its way from Dublin and a rapparee, one of a number of freelance outlaws of the period, called 'Galloping' Hogan was able to advise Sarsfield of its progress, especially of its bivouac at Ballyneety, six miles south of the city.

With Hogan to guide them 600 of Sarsfield's finest cavalry were able to attack the train. They headed out in a wide clockwise arc crossing the Shannon at Killaloe and approaching the Williamite camp with muffled hooves. One of the folk legends associated with the episode is that the watchword for the sentinels at Ballyneety was 'Sarsfield', information Sarsfield obtained from his spies. The story goes that when challenged by sentries, he cried, 'Sarsfield is the watchword – Sarsfield is the man.' He and his companions were able to carry away the already harnessed horses, dig the cannon muzzles into the earth and heap the barrels of explosive into a pile that exploded with a sound that was audible in Limerick. It meant a delay in attacking the town of ten days as another siege train was brought from Waterford.

William was anxious to get back to the Netherlands to the *real* war against France. He decided on 27 August to mount a frontal attack against Irishtown, where the walls were especially weak. The town had 14,000 inhabitants and under the governor, the Marquis de Boisseleau, they were determined to hold out; even the women stood ready with hand-sized stones and broken bottles. After four hours of intense fighting and the loss of 2000 of his best men William withdrew. He thought to prolong the action by siege but he had not sufficient men entirely to surround the town and was conscious of the onset of autumn and the effect of heavy rains on the unmetalled roads. He called off the siege and brought his troops to winter quarters in Dublin, where a further 2000 would die of disease. His departure from Ireland shortly afterwards enabled Sarsfield, now the recognised Irish leader, to clear the Williamites from Connacht and secure the towns of Galway, Limerick, Sligo and, most importantly, Athlone. The Jacobites would live to fight another day.

THE SIEGE OF KINSALE
29 SEPTEMBER-15 OCTOBER 1690

The battle of the Boyne, however cherished and celebrated in Protestant memory, was only part of a war that lasted for more than two years. The subjugation of south Munster was entrusted to the Earl (not yet Duke) of Marlborough (1650-1722) and the Duke of Würtemburg-Neustadt, sharing command on alternate days, an odd imposition by William III (1650-1702) that required great tact and forbearance. The king distrusted Marlborough and the other English officers and felt more at home with the Danes, Dutch and French Huguenots who were Boyne veterans.

The task of the leaders was to capture Cork and Kinsale, the two ports that were the main sources of French military supplies. An expedition of eighty-two ships sailed up the River Lee on 30 August 1690, landing Marlborough on the south bank and Scravenmoer on the north. The Duke of Grafton was assigned a man-o'-war that he generously renamed *Grafton* and attacked what little defences Cork had. He was mortally wounded while setting his naval guns but there were others to continue the bombardment. The seaborne cannonballs made a breach on the east wall and the two forces north and south occupied the city with little resistance.

The little town of Kinsale that had been so significant in Irish history nearly a century before is seventeen miles from Cork. It was guarded by two forts where the River Bandon bends into Kinsale Harbour, the one on the west on a spur of land overlooking the town, called the Old or James Fort, the other now called Charles Fort, then new and virtually unassailable. The town was otherwise unprotected and Marlborough's cavalry, led by Colonel Villiers, took possession without delay, on 29 September 1690. Malborough then ordered the Danish Major-General Tattau to seize the Old Fort with 600 fusiliers and 200 grenadiers. The troops crossed the river at Inishannon at dawn on 2 October and after fierce resistance by the 400 Irish defenders drove them into the centre of the fort where the gunpowder was stored. They had to surrender when this store blew up, killing Colonel O'Driscoll and forty of the Irish soldiers.

The New Fort was pentagonal in shape with a deep dry moat all the way round and only one drawbridge and gate. Defence systems were concentrated here and when Tattau began to dig trenches on 3 October Irish sorties delayed the work. The weather was wet and very windy, preventing the Williamite artillery from arriving by sea; cavalry horses were used to drag six cannon and two mortars overland from Cork and these were finally in position by 12 October. The guns were set up on high ground to the south of the fort, the mortars further round to the south-east. After hard pounding from both sections for more than two days a breach was finally made in the east wall. By 15 October Sir Edward Scott, who had earlier dismissed any suggestion of surrender as too early by a month, had to agree that 'the fort be handed over intact, that the officers should retain their swords and that both garrison and the Catholic inhabitants have safe conduct to some place of security'. The garrison of 1000 men marched out and headed for Limerick to carry on the fight while Brigadier Charles Churchill, Marlborough's brother, was appointed governor of Kinsale.

AUGHRIM
12 JULY 1691

After the unnecessary débâcle at the Boyne the Irish Jacobites fell
back to fortress Connacht. They held Sligo, Limerick and Athlone
and had the Shannon as a long defensive outer moat. Louis XIV
of France was still anxious to help James, his guest, and James's
Irish supporters for his own purposes, since England, their enemy
and his, was the most active member of the anti-French coalition
known as the League of Augsburg. Men and supplies from France
could be landed at Galway and the other coastal towns. After the
departure of the two kings, for reasons of efficiency and respect,
the anti-Jacobite allies accepted Godert de Ginkel (1630-1703),
William III's crack Dutch general, as commander-in-chief, while
the Irish and French acquiesced in Charles Chalmont, Marquis de
St Ruth (d. 1691) more reluctantly. So strong was the dissension
between Tyrconnell (1630-91) James II's viceroy and Patrick
Sarsfield (*c.* 1650-93), the native Irish leader, that Louis XIV
appointed St Ruth as overall commander.

Ginkel's army, the victor of the Boyne, was fully mobilised
and moved against Athlone before St Ruth had fully assembled
his motley troops, comprising trained French and Irish soldiers,
aristocratic Irish cavalry, conscripts from among the tenantry of
Irish landlords and some freelance rapparees. Most of Ginkel's
troops were Protestant from the northern European states: they
included Danes, Dutch, French Huguenots expelled from France,
Scots Presbyterians and Ulster Protestants. As well as having
military efficiency they were imbued with an almost religious

elation that made them very determined fighters.

William III had realised the tactical importance of Athlone in 1690 but failed to take the town. The bridge in the town was the most convenient, if not the only, means of crossing the Shannon into Connacht. When St Ruth ordered it to be destroyed Ginkel's men were sent to rebuild it, although they were continually under fire. St Ruth had brought with him thirty-six cannon along with six mortars when he landed at Limerick on 9 May 1691 and these he trained on Ginkel's engineers when he reached the town on 19 June. The Williamites had occupied the English section of the town but could make little headway into the Irish part, where the Jacobites had dug in. After a week of constant artillery fire Ginkel's scouts reported a possible ford not far upstream and the crack Dutch troops were sent to cross it and attack the Jacobites' rear. There was great slaughter but eventually Ginkel took the town and began to plan for the final putsch against St Ruth and Patrick Sarsfield.

St Ruth chose to draw up his troops on Kilcommodam Hill above the village of Aughrim, sixteen miles south-west of Athlone. Sarsfield argued strongly against a pitched battle there, knowing that the Irish troops were inexperienced and feeling that a defence of Limerick was the best tactic. He was overruled and placed in charge of the cavalry on the left flank, where he joined the best of St Ruth's infantry. When he landed in Limerick St Ruth had brought with him 16,000 infantry, 3000 light cavalry and 2000 dragoons – as the heavily armoured cavalry were then called, as well as arms, ammunition, food and clothing. Now on 5 July he awaited the coming of Ginkel's army that was camped at Ballinasloe five miles to the north-east. The hill was an ideal position for a battle, with an extensive bog at its foot and the hill itself plotted with stone ditches and thick hedges that made ideal cover for the raw Irish soldiers. There were only two viable causeways through the bog and one of these was guarded by Aughrim Castle. St Ruth's total force was about 20,000 and it seemed that he held all the cards.

Early on 12 July, a Sunday morning, Ginkel advanced from Ballinasloe with approximately the same number of troops. At the first sign of his advance the Jacobite outposts left their positions, crossed the bog and took up new positions behind the stone ditches. The battle proper began at 1pm. The first attack was frontal but the Jacobite line held and there were so many casualties among the French Huguenots who formed the vanguard that the grass was slippery with blood and the place is still known locally as the 'Bloody Hollow'. The Williamites were driven back after three forays. It became clear to Ginkel that, the bog being unforceable, a passage would have to be made by the causeway on St Ruth's left. It should have been impregnable but the Jacobites were running low on ammunition and found that their British bullets did not fit the muzzles of their French muskets. Aughrim village soon fell to the Williamites.

There was still a force of Jacobite cavalry under Brigadier Henry Luttrell (*c.* 1655-1717) that could have prevented Williamite incursion except that Luttrell ordered them to withdraw instead of attack. The causeway is still known as Luttrell's Pass and most people believe that he was in Ginkel's pay. After Limerick he brought his regiment into the Williamite army and as a reward was given back his family estate in County Dublin and an annual pension of £500. His death at the hands of an assassin–he was shot in his sedan chair in Stafford Street (now Wolfe Tone Street) in Dublin on 3 November 1717– was not thought to be connected with his military career.

At about the same time that the Jacobites' weakness was revealed at Luttrell's Pass their morale plummeted; it had become clear that the commander-in-chief had been killed in a gruesome way, decapitated by a cannonball. The ominous and unthinkable nature of St Ruth's end made the superstitious foot soldiers run away from the centre and as they fled west they were slaughtered by Ginkel's cavalry. They threw away their weapons to help them run faster but cavalry horses easily overtook them. An eyewitness said that the hill was covered with bodies like flocks of grazing sheep. There were casualties on both sides; the Williamites had lost many men in the battle of the bog. The total death toll was in excess of 7000, more than half of these being Jacobites. Four thousand Jacobites were taken prisoner or deserted.

Aughrim was the last and bloodiest of the 'great' Irish battles, known in Irish, the language of most of the people then, as *Eachdhroim an Áir* ('Aughrim of the slaughter'). Poignantly recalled in a ballad by Canon P.A. Sheehan (1852-1913): 'After Aughrim's great disaster/When the foe in sooth were master...' It was the real defeat of James II's hopes; Galway fell without resistance on 21 July and Limerick was a siege of last hope. Since it was the greatest Jacobite defeat it was celebrated as such by Loyalists until the early nineteenth century, especially by the Orange Order from its founding in 1795. From the Order's point of view, however, it lacked the great icon; Ginkel had not the grandeur or the glamour of King Billy. And so the Boyne, where the Jacobites were assumed to have acted in a cowardly fashion, replaced Aughrim in the calendar of Irish Protestantism.

THE SECOND SIEGE OF LIMERICK
30 AUGUST-23 SEPTEMBER 1691

After the fall of Galway, Count Godert de Ginkel (1630-1703), the Williamite commander, turned his attention to Limerick, the Jacobites' last citadel. The breach in the Irishtown wall had been repaired and earthworks, more useful even than the walls, had been built up behind them. Unlike William III, Ginkel's concentration was total; he was determined to end Jacobitism. Persuaded by Patrick Sarsfield the Jacobites decided again to defend the town, although their morale had been badly affected by the sudden death of the Earl of Tyrconnell (1630-91), James's viceroy, many believed by poison, and the court-martial of Brigadier Henry Luttrell (c. 1655-1717) for treason after the Battle of Aughrim.

Ginkel, like William, had to wait for artillery of sufficient firepower before he could attack the city. It was not until 30 August that the cannon were in position and ready to fire. Failing to breach the Irishtown defences, Ginkel turned his attention to the weaker Englishtown to the east. A new battery was ready by 8 September and Ginkel set it to attack the walls. He then had his engineers build floats to take his assault troops across the Abbey River, a tributary of the Shannon. This ploy was countered by a move by a Jacobite commando who destroyed most of the floats the next night. The artillery kept pounding until the breach in the Englishtown walls was widened to forty feet, leaving the town vulnerable to a force landing on the north shore. On 15 September Ginkel began to build a pontoon bridge a quarter of a mile upstream, with the intention of blockading the city while effectively giving him a means of crossing the river. The fact that he succeeded was due to inattention if not actual carelessness on the part of the cavalry based on the Clare side of the river.

On 16 September Ginkel offered generous surrender terms to the city, along with a dire warning of terror after eight days, should his terms not be accepted. By 22 September the bridge was ready and Ginkel poured most of his army across to the Clare side. They quickly overcame the force from Irishtown sent against them. As the Jacobite force retreated towards Thomond Bridge and the safety of Englishtown they found that the drawbridge had been raised prematurely by a French major, who was afraid that the enemy would capture the bridge. Those left outside were butchered, too tightly packed to defend themselves. Some were pushed towards the gap into the river or fell over the sides and drowned. Some tried to surrender but received no quarter. In all 600 men were lost in the brief encounter and of these about 150 were drowned. The events of that day changed the situation totally and influenced the course of Irish history for the next hundred years.

When the garrison officers met that night and the bitter recriminations over the raising of the drawbridge by the French temporarily ceased, discussion turned to the possibility of seeking a honourable truce. The garrison was isolated, the promised French ship had not materialised and relations between the French and the Irish acrimonious. The best they could hope for was a truce as offered earlier by Ginkel. In the afternoon of 23 September a parley was sounded by Irish drums and Limerick, betrayed by the victors, would soon become known as the 'City of the Broken Treaty'.

CARRICKFERGUS
21 FEBRUARY 1760

The Seven Years War (1756-63) between Britain and France had campaigns all over the shrinking world – in India, the Mediterranean, the West Indies, Canada – and a brief episode in County Antrim.

Carrickfergus Castle had been built in 1177 by John de Courcy, the freelance Anglo-Norman lord of Ulster, when Belfast was just a sandbank. It had seen much history in succeeding centuries and played its part, too, in a daring raid by Commodore François Thurot, a French freebooter during that country's war with England. Thurot was born at Nuits Saint-George near Dijon on 22 July 1727 and was at sea from an early age. He was imprisoned for a year in Dover, where he learned to speak excellent English, until he escaped in a stolen boat. In 1748 he managed to gather enough money to provision a merchant ship. The next seven years were spent partly in England but mainly in smuggling and piracy. He had made such a name for himself as a daring captain that by the outbreak of the war he was made commander of a squadron of seven frigates and a cutter, rapid response ships that harried the shipping off the east coast of England.

On 21 February 1760 he steered his squadron into Belfast Lough and anchored at Kilroot, two miles north-east of Carrickfergus. A landing party of 600 men, well fortified with rum, was sent on longboats, the eighteenth-century equivalent of landing craft, to capture the castle. The defence of the town was in the charge of Lieutenant-General John Jennings, who had 170 'other ranks', twenty-one NCOs and five officers, who in the true tradition of military farce were half a mile down the Belfast road on an exercise when Thurot's landing party reached the shore. Jennings ordered his men to resist the invaders on the beach while he transported 100 French prisoners under the guard of a local 'pressed' militia to Belfast.

The castle guard were English, who compensated for a crucial lack of ball and gunpowder with bricks and stones. The ornately costumed Redcoats cut the brass buttons from their greatcoats to use as bullets. The garrison put up a fierce fight but without sufficient arms Jennings was forced to seek a truce. The garrison would evacuate the castle with full honours of war. The officers, consisting of two lieutenants and three ensigns, were to be paroled in Ireland and the 'men' exchanged for French prisoners. The store of gunpowder was dumped in the lough and the cannon spiked. Jennings had lost only three men while the casualty list among the French was at least thirty-six and perhaps as much as sixty.

The taking of Carrickfergus had taken nine hours. The intruders stayed for a week, glad of unexpected shore leave, and returned to their ships only when the three regiments of reinforcements hurried from Dublin arrived on 27 February. The whole affair was so daring as to demand a happy ending but Thurot and his squadron were attacked next morning by a superior naval force off the Isle of Man. Thurot was killed, his ships destroyed and twenty-three officers and 409 sailors and marines taken prisoner.

THE DIAMOND
21 SEPTEMBER 1795

The Diamond is a rather grand title for a hamlet near a crossroads less than two miles north of Loughgall in County Armagh. It was a centre for farmer-weavers with a pub owned by Dan Winter, known for different reasons as 'Diamond Dan' and 'Orange Dan'. The first name was simply topographical, the second a clear mark of his allegiance. Before he became king, William III (1650-1702) was correctly known as William, Prince of Orange, a principality in the Dutch republic. From the coming of the Hanoverian kings his name was used iconically 'to defend the ould cause/That gave us our freedom, religion and laws,' as the song put it.

The last decade of the eighteenth century was a time of political turmoil, not only in France, where the revolution was in full spate, but in Ulster, where the existence of the Society of United Irishmen was regarded by the local aristocracy and magistracy as proof of Presbyterian disloyalty. The underclass Catholics were neither God-fearing Anglicans nor revolutionary Presbyterians and the old atavistic fear dating back to 1641 meant that they were by no means to be trusted or permitted to bear arms.

By 1795, however, Ulster Catholics had gathered enough self-confidence to find defensive arms and to benefit from wartime prices for the linen that they manufactured in their cottage industries. The Protestants of north Armagh resented this economic success even more than their political presumption and campaigns of terror that would later have been called pogroms were frequently employed against Catholics. The more militant among the catholics formed secret societies called generally 'Defenders'. Their opponents named themselves 'Orange Boys' or 'Peep O'Day Boys' from their subtle habit of the early-morning raids of Catholic houses looking for arms, which were strictly speaking not forbidden unless the local magistrate decided otherwise. In Protestant eyes Catholics had become as great a menace as they were a century and a half earlier in the rising of 1641.

In June 1795 the fair day in Loughgall had been the scene of a sectarian riot; unease and smouldering watchfulness characterised the rest of the troubled summer. Local Protestants became greatly alarmed when they learned on 21 September that at 5.00 am about 500 local Defenders had gathered on Tartaraghan Hill, south of the Diamond. Fearing for their lives and property they called on the local chapter of the Peep O'Days for help and these obligingly assembled on Cragnagill Hill on the other side of the Tall River, In an initial confrontation one Defender was killed. After that both sides stayed on the opposing hills shooting across at each other, with little effect because of the distance between them.

The local gentry and clergy, alarmed at the noise, met hurriedly at Crowhill House, the home of Joseph Atkinson JP. He went as surety of £50 (£3000 in today's purchasing power) for the Protestant gang while three Catholic priests offered the same surety for their flock. A document of agreement was drawn up but the Defenders, elated at a kind of victory and steadily reinforced from the surrounding countryside, refused to be bound by it. They advanced towards Faughert Fort on a hill immediately above the Diamond. In the mêlée that followed Dan Winter's inn was fired and his store of liquor, tea and flour were thrown on to the road. He and his sons escaped with their lives by squeezing through a narrow window and ran uphill through an orchard, one of many for which the county is famous. They were pursued by a band of Defenders who turned and fled when they realised that a party of Peep O'Days, known even then as 'Orange Boys' and les by the fearsome James 'Buddra' Wilson was about to charge them.

At the Diamond proper fierce hand-to-hand fighting followed and in the true 'Battle of the Diamond' the Defenders were soon vanquished, the proceedings barely lasting half-an-hour.

Opinions differ as to the number of fatalities. John Mitchel (1815-75), the stern Unitarian Young Irelander, dismissed the Battle of the Diamond as trivial, another typical fracas of the time, in which no more than 'four or five Defenders were killed or wounded; and this is the glorious battle that had been toasted at Orange banquets from that day to the present.' The actual number of dead Defenders was about thirty but Mitchel was correct in his dismissal of its glorification by succeeding generations and fear of its long-lasting aftermath: from that crossroads confrontation sprang the Orange Order, an organisation that has proved to be miraculously strong and intermittently menacing. When the pursuit of the retreating Catholics was finally abandoned, a number of the exultant victors stained with blood and gunpowder, gathered in a field close to the burnt-out liquor house and, joining hands in a circle round a small bush, vowed to form a new defensive fraternity. They adjourned to Winter's home to discuss the idea and called a fuller meeting that evening in a pub in Loughgall, owned by James Sloan. Present were 'Buddra' Wilson, Dan Winter, John Dilly, Nicholas Lockhart, Robert Irwin, George Templeton and James Sloan. Also in the company was Captain John Giffard of the Dublin Royal Militia, who is credited with drawing up the rules and structures of the new order that 'for generations would crib both pope and popery in Ireland'. Winter was appropriately the first member inducted, with water from a well in his own garden.

THE RISING OF 1798

CARLOW
25 MAY 1798

The rebellion of the United Irishmen in 1798 that convulsed the south-east, north-east and west of Ireland manifested itself in a total of twenty eruptions and skirmishes. It could have been a significant part of Napoleon's plan to invade England had not chance and Ireland's weather defeated the French hope of landing a formidable army at Bantry Bay in December 1796. Gales made it impossible for the ships to dock and England was saved by a hurricane, as in 1588 when 'God blew and they [the Spanish Armada] were scattered.' Wolfe Tone (1763-98) would try for French aid again with even less success and for the most of the remainder of the decade Irish nationalists continued to cherish for their homeland the hope that: 'The French are on the way.'

The United Irishmen were formed out of a conviction that the Irish government was partial, venal and selfish, even though in Henry Grattan (1746-1820) the parliament had at least one man of integrity. Members were greatly influenced by the French Revolution that had begun in 1789, some cutting their hair short in emulation of the Jacobins and earning the name of 'Croppies'. Throughout the latter part of the 1790s membership grew, carefully monitored by British and Irish authorities–for there were many informers. Local regiments of volunteers known as 'yeomen', largely composed of members of the recently formed Orange Order, were formed to impose virtual martial law.

There were outbreaks of rebellion on 23-24 May 1798 in Meath, Dublin and Kildare and Carlow. The subsequent Carlow incident was typical of others that would follow. In the early morning of 25 May the local rebels assembled outside the town. Country people, they had come from different parts of the county – Grange, Hacketstown, Tullow and Leighlin – and intended to rendezvous with a contingent from the adjacent Queen's County (Laois) at Graigue Bridge. The leader of the substantial force of perhaps 1200 was a young shoemaker called Michael Heydon. Two hundred of them marched without opposition towards the Potato Market in the town. It was early in the morning, still quiet, and Heydon did realise that he had marched into a well-planned ambush. With a mixture of enthusiasm and naïveté characteristic of the time he believed that not only the largely Catholic militia but the sectarian Yeomen would rally to the rebels. The soldiers of the garrison were concealed behind the windows of the buildings and raked the crowds of unprotected rebels in the market. Those who were not shot rushed on to get away from the musket fire and ran straight into another ambush. If any survivor managed to take refuge in house or cabin the soldiers set fire to the building, thereby causing the deaths of 200 of the townsfolk. A local witness described how a townsman ran out of his house carrying his young daughter: 'He was instantly shot dead and his daughter'.

An estimated 600 people lay dead and rebels who had survived were betrayed by an informer called 'Paddy the Pointer', who helped identify them to the military by ranging round the town and pointing them out. This resulted in further repression and the executions of another 150 people. The dead were collected and buried in a mass grave still known as the Croppy Hole.

Antrim
7 June 1798

In many ways the insurrection of 1798 originated in Ulster; it was in the small intensely radical eighteenth-century town of Belfast that the Society of United Irishmen first came into being. In the presence of Wolfe Tone the secret society's oath was solemnised on top of Cave Hill. Their newspaper the *Northern Star* (1792-7) had been very popular under its editor Samuel Neilson (1761-1803) until its offices and machinery were destroyed by a band of Monaghan militia, a notoriously drunken and undisciplined force. Defenders (as the Catholics called their defensive organisations) played little part in the northern insurrection, in contrast to that of the south-east. As in the rest of the country, however, government spies had infiltrated most of the lodges and were assiduous in these duties. A young Catholic, Nicholas Mageean, kept the authorities informed of the plans of the intended risings both in Antrim and in Down.

The most charismatic Ulster leader was Henry Joy McCracken (1767-98), the ineffectual manager of a family cotton business and one of the original founders of the United Irishmen. He had spent most of 1797 in Kilmainham Gaol but was unregenerate in his conviction that insurrection was the only road to the liberty he worshipped more than life. Arms had been assembled and many young men, some of them clerical students, were ready to revolt. Older and wiser counsels refused to move without some sign of French support but the younger members insisted that they rise without delay and appointed McCracken as commander. He knew that an attack on heavily garrisoned Belfast with its strictly enforced curfew was pointless; he was also aware through his sister Mary Anne (1770-1866) that even among Belfast radicals support for the French revolution, then in the grip of the 'Terror', had ceased. On the whole, the town of Antrim, seventeen miles away on the roads to Derry and Ballymena, was a better, more useful target. McCracken spread the word throughout the north that the great push for liberty was about to begin. He urged the various branches in South Antrim to make their moves in Templepatrick, Larne and Ballymena, securing these virtually undefended towns. He also called for as large a force as possible to muster on Donegore Hill, three miles east of Antrim town.

On the morning of 7 June word came that the republicans had taken the town of Larne and had begun to set up in Ballymena a Committee of Public Safety, along the lines of similar agencies in France in the early days of the revolution. All seemed well but McCracken did not know that General Nugent, commander of all the English forces in the North, was aware of every detail of his plans. Nugent was in something of a quandary: he dared not move too many troops from Belfast in case of a spontaneous rising there and was therefore obliged to take a calculated risk and summon a mixed force of regulars, dragoons, 'Yeos' and militia (a suspect force with most other ranks Papist) in two columns, one from Belfast and the other from Lisburn. Randalstown fell to the rebels without a shot being fired and by midday they seemed in control of most of south Antrim, a circle of twenty miles in diameter measured from Glenarm on the coast to Toomebridge at the head of Lough Neagh. McCracken still waited, as if reluctant to enter the town of Antrim, even though at mid-morning his army greatly outnumbered all the townspeople. When at two in the afternoon he finally made his move, the garrison under Colonel Durham was ready for the rebels. Already a strong force of dragoons was racing from the south and their young commander, Colonel William Lumley, made the mistake of charging a group of rebels armed with long pikes. It was an error that had also been made to the detriment of dragoons in Wicklow, Kildare and Wexford and resulted in the deaths of a third of the troop.

The more experienced Colonel Durham pounded the town with artillery before sending in his infantry as Durham held part of Antrim. The Monaghan Militia, already with a fierce reputation, further blackened their name by shooting *loyalist* citizens, running out to welcome them as saviours. Although McCracken held a good part of the town, fighting continued as he impatiently waited for support from Samuel Orr's Randalstown contingent, which was marching the six miles from the west. These men were also inexplicably late and when they did enter the town by the west gate they were met by a charge of dragoons in retreat. Orr's men mistakenly assumed that they were being attacked by the dragoons and scattered, the volunteers managing to go to ground in a remarkably short time. Without Orr's support McCracken was forced to retreat and began to withdraw from the town. News quickly reached the camp at Donegore that Antrim had not been the easy operation they had expected. The crowd of over 3000 men gradually slipped away.

McCracken made his way east and was sheltered in Collin Glen in the countryside west of Belfast. He then made his way to Cave Hill outside Belfast. He should have been safe in hiding there while his sister Mary Anne tried to find him a berth on a ship for America. It was pure chance that caused the Carrickfergus Yeomanry to find him on 8 July. He refused to name his comrades and was hanged in the Cornmarket in Belfast nine days later.

ARKLOW
9 JUNE 1798

The most significant battles of the 1798 rebellion took place in Wexford, where the insurgents had some successes, buoyed up by news of supposed gains in Wicklow and Kildare. In fact the risings there were put down with extreme cruelties by the British army supplemented by enthusiastic band of Yeomen, militia (especially the infamous North Cork) and sectarian volunteers, mainly members of the recently formed Orange Order. In a sense it was the extreme anticipatory force shown by the army, with unauthorised burning of cottages, killing of women and children and application of the appalling pitch-cap to untried prisoners that increased the resolve of the republicans. Two significant prelates, Father John Murphy and Father Michael Murphy, reluctantly assumed leadership, mainly to prevent outrages from their own people, and the first of these is commemorated by the famous ballad, 'Boolavogue' written by Patrick Joseph McCall (1861-1919) in the comparative peace and security of 1898, to celebrate the centenary of the revolt. It is thanks to McCall that such place names as Shelmalier, Kilcormack, Camolin, Enniscorthy, New Ross, Gorey, Killane and Vinegar Hill and the battles associated with them were made familiar to succeeding generations of Irish people.

Because of the fear that the self-sacrificing elation of the United Irishmen would affect the whole country and the terror of a French invasion while Napoleon, the great Satan, was in power, a policy of frightfulness was at first condoned and later ordered by the authorities. Later on, when the victorious army drove the rebels back, they had no concern for the reprisals inflicted on peaceful loyalists. The names that live in infamy are Scullabogue, where 200 loyalist prisoners crowded into a barn were mercilessly butchered and Wexford town, where ninety Protestants were taken out and executed. These atrocities, however, were minimal compared with those inflicted, especially by the 'Yeos', after every victory or defeat. The rebels were fairly disciplined while their numbers in arms were small but when the 'French disease', as John Thomas Troy (1739-1823), Catholic Archbishop of Dublin, described it, was at its height and the numbers of willing volunteers at their greatest it was difficult to control them or delete the memories of a century of persecution.

The insurrection was most successful in what would soon have been the independent republican state of Wexford. The rebels held most of the county south of Gorey and, although lacking both a clear united policy and an effective command structure, as well as being woefully short of arms except the ubiquitous pike, might have beaten off the British. The idea of moving in to Wicklow and capturing Arklow seemed to some the next logical step, especially to the Wicklow leaders who were part of the rebel command. They were on a road that led directly to Dublin and they were surely not going to stay in the south-east. Father John Murphy, one of the Wexford captains, tried to dissuade the rebels from leaving the comparative safety of the county they knew. While debates about the next move continued heatedly in the Gorey camp the enemy used the delay to reoccupy the town.

Arklow suited the rebels' suicidal tactics of facing muskets and cannon with pikes and the sheer weight of numbers. Suggestions that the town could be by-passed on the east, if necessary by fording the notoriously shallow and tidal River Avoca, made especially passable by the droughty summer of 1798, were ignored. Orders had come from some of the leaders for a frontal attack and they would be adhered to. There was a further delay while a large body of republicans was winkled out of a liquor store.

This was an unfortunate feature of several battles, causing Robert Dwyer Joyce (1830-83) to include in his famous ballad 'The Boys of Wexford' a verse about the dire effects of alcohol:

> *We bravely fought and conquered at Ross and Wexford town*
> *And if we failed to keep them, 'twas drink that brought us down.*

The soldiers in the town of Arklow were on parade and were startled at the sight of thousands (some said 19,000) of pikemen suddenly appearing on ditches and crowded upon the sandbanks around the town. They levelled their pikes and charged in spite of being raked by grapeshot from five pieces of ordnance. Some advanced right to the mouths of cannon, to the reluctant admiration of General Francis Needham, who was in overall command. They managed to break through in at least one salient and set that part of the town on fire. They had little chance, however, against the discipline and firepower of the British fencibles. The rebels withstood two and a half hours of heavy artillery pounding, then fled, pursued by dragoons who were able to use their sabres to dire effect. After the battle the field was covered with broken pikes and pitchforks – and up to three hundred corpses. There were also the sad rags of green flags inscribed 'Liberty or Death' and those amulets against fate, Catholic scapulars. Afraid that his store of ammunition might run out, Needham ordered a ceasefire and this enabled the intrepid insurgents to collect nine cartloads of wounded and flee with them back south to Gorey so that they could be patched up and with replenished ammunition carry on the fight. A prominent victim of the Arklow venture was Father Michael Murphy of Ballycanew, who fell at the very end of the battle and whose body was subject to the usual indignities.

BALLYNAHINCH
13 JUNE 1798

By all tactical calculations the rising in Down should have happened several days earlier than it did to coincide with that in Antrim. Then General Nugent should have had a serious problem of troop allocation. As it was he felt he was risking the safety of Belfast by sending a relief force to defeat McCracken. Since the rising in Antrim collapsed in a matter of days it was with greater confidence that Nugent led the same kind of composite force out along the Long Bridge over the mud flats of the Lagan. The reasons for the lack of simultaneous action were several: characteristic lack of communicated intelligence; confusion about leadership; and reluctance on the part of the designated commanders to move without the physical presence of the long-promised French support. Nicholas Mageean, the government's ubiquitous mole, had already delivered to Nugent a full account of the rebels' strength, disposition and plan of campaign and the authorities were able to arrest the Reverend William Steele Jackson (a local United Irishman) on 5 June. The republicans in Down were as ready as their comrades in Antrim but no one seemed to have considered that simultaneous risings would have been much more effective.

When the word flashed round the north of the county that Antrim was 'up' it was not long until the Down republicans controlled the Ards peninsula and most of the Lecale peninsula, with Newtownards, Bangor, Comber, Saintfield and Ballynahinch under temporary revolutionary control. Newtownards had fallen to the rebels after the famous 'Pike Sunday' (10 June) sermon by the Reverend Thomas Leslie Birch of Saintfield First Presbyterian Church, which urged revolt. This early success helped to persuade Henry Monroe (1758-98), a native of Scotland, who worked in a linen draper's shop in the Market Square in Lisburn, to accept the leadership of the 'United Army of Down'. His job entailed travelling around the linen halls of Lurgan, Banbridge and Tanderagee buying webs for the bleachers, so he was well known throughout the county. He was a Freemason, head of the Lisburn lodge, and had joined the Volunteers in 1778, holding the honorary rank of adjutant. He was well thought of but had no real experience of military tactics, having been a mere member of the United army that he joined in 1795. A man of lofty ideals, he was very deeply concerned to prevent indiscriminate violence and looting by his untrained force and anxious that they should not inflict damage on the extensive estates of Francis Rawdon-Hasting, Lord Moira, at Montalto, near Ballynahinch, because Moira was a noted supporter of Catholic Emancipation. He refused to take possession of Ballynahinch after the egregious Monaghan militia had caused considerable damage in their characteristically drunken and predatory way and thought it ungallant to move against Nugent's forces during the night. He had sent his best soldiers to the town, where they established themselves on Windmill Hill, but they were soon dislodged from there by regulars, a company of Fyfe and Argyll fencibles led by Colonel Stewart, who had marched north-west from Downpatrick. He nevertheless decided that the town's narrow winding streets would suit his long-pikemen in close conflict.

During the evening of 12 June Nugent's small but effective party of cannoneers arrived with their ordnance and began to attack the town from the west. This caused many of the rebels to desert with their arms, seriously weakening Monroe's force, which had already lost many Catholic 'Defenders', who felt that they were running extra danger of capture and death, a fear not shared by their Presbyterian allies. With the coming of a grey summer dawn and the promise of a fine day Monroe set his eager troops to attack the Belfast and Downpatrick contingents. As he had anticipated his pikemen easily repulsed Nugent's cavalry and sent them running towards the edge of the town. Their commander had his bugler sound the retreat. Monroe's men, unacquainted with British army trumpet calls, assumed it was a signal to charge and turned back, believing that they were about to face a fresh attack. They began to retreat themselves, only to be cut down by the reinvigorated cavalry and the two cannon brought by Stewart from Downpatrick.

In the ensuing slaughter 400 of the United army were killed, while British losses amounted to no more than forty. Nugent's order to the 22nd Dragoons: 'Now, boys, be merciful,' was completely ignored; it probably was tongue-in-cheek anyway and certainly no mercy was shown to the rebels or any unfortunate townspeople who were caught in the charge. Two days later Monroe was captured, court-martialled and sentenced to death. With exquisite tact his gallows were set up in the Market Square opposite his home, giving a grandstand view to his wife and sisters. He was later decapitated and his head spiked as a warning to others.

The battle of Ballynahinch, otherwise inglorious, had a slight element of romance about it in that one of protagonists was an Ulster Joan of Arc. She was Betsy Grey (c. 1778-98) a beautiful twenty-year-old who rode into battle on a pure white steed, dressed in green (according to the later prints), and chased the vile Monaghan Militia for their lives. She, her brother George and her lover Willie Boal tried to organise the retreat, although they could have escaped, They were met on the road by a party of Hillsborough Yeomanry who shot the two men but as Betsy fought on her right hand was severed and she was shot through the eye. She later became the subject of many ballads and had a column of black oak erected in her honour in 1898.

VINEGAR HILL
21 JUNE 1798

The battle of Vinegar Hill (and nearby Enniscorthy) was essentially the last hurrah of the rising in Wexford although it did not mean the absolute annihilation of the United Irishmen forces in that county. The site was not chosen as a battleground; it was rather a kind of base camp where women and children as well as combatants had taken refuge. Because of its steep elevation, with excellent views of the surrounding countryside and the town of Enniscorthy, it was considered a suitable gathering place for the United soldiers but with its usual accurate intelligence the Crown forces decided to make it the final confrontation. A total of 20,000 republicans assembled there and there was a sense even among the most sanguine of a last glorious stand for their republican ideals.

General Gerard Lake, the British commander, divided his 18,000 men into four sections, each led by a general. Three of the sections, led by Dundas, Duff and Needham, were to obliterate the force on Vinegar Hill, the fourth led by Johnson to mop up any residual opposition in the town of Enniscorthy. It took a long time for the cumbersome machinery of war to get ready and Needham's column was not in position when Lake gave orders for the attack. The republican defenders had little in the way of arms except their pikes, deadly to charging cavalry but matchsticks in the face of the artillery that was dragged forward with every inch of ground gained. The republican troops were gradually compressed into an ever-tightening circle. Some of the wilder ones raced to face the cannon on at least two occasions and briefly delayed the relentless progress of the Crown forces. As it was, almost 1000, including women and children, were sabred, shot or blown to pieces by cannon shell but incredibly about 19,000 escaped. The dilatory Needham was late in arriving and the greater majority of the republican fighters escaped downhill through what is still known as Needham's Gap.

Johnson had not done very well in Enniscorthy. There was fierce resistance by republicans led by William Barker and, without artillery and unused to 'hand-to-hand', the Crown forces were unable to take the bridge. The republicans were relieved by a contingent of newly arrived comrades from South Wexford who held the bridge and allowed the streams of refugees from the hill to reach the east bank of the Slaney and safety. When Lake realised that the rebels were retreating he released the cavalry on the stragglers and ordered his artillerymen to fire grapeshot to maximise the injuries. The usual scenes of violence followed and a hospital in Enniscorthy was set on fire. Father John Murphy 'of old Kilcormack' was found asleep in a barn and after the customary indignities and torture was hanged and beheaded. Vinegar Hill was not the end of action by the republicans as a successful raid at Ballyellis on 30 June showed but there were no more pitched battles. As the ballad laments: 'The gold sun of freedom grew darkened at Ross and was set by the Slaney's red waves.' The dead were buried in shallow graves on the hill and the following summer the wheat in their pockets sprouted into ripeness. The event gave a potent symbol of hope to the Irish and to Seamus Heaney a theme for a poem.

The 'Races' of Castlebar
27 August 1798

On 22 August 1798, when Ireland seemed in the eyes of the government to have been at last all but pacified, 'the ships we'd been wearily waiting sailed into Killala's broad bay.' To quote from an earlier ballad, the West was suddenly and thrillingly awake. Three French frigates were anchored off Kilcummin Strand at the north-west tip of Killala Bay in County Mayo. 1100 French soldiers landed without opposition and soon had Killala under their control. The larger town of Ballina at the head of the lough fell two days later. Their commander was the dashing young General Jean-Joseph Amable Humbert and he should have been the vanguard of a much larger force of 9000 veteran troops led by General Hardy. As with every attempt to land significant foreign support in Ireland from the sixteenth century on, the weather favoured the British. General Hardy's fleet was forced to return to France.

The Irish of Connacht, hearing of the French 'invasion', came in numbers to join Ireland's latest and last hope. The French were amused and appalled at the indiscipline and political naïveté of the Irish, especially these men of the west, but they could not deny their willingness to fight. Any available government forces were ordered to proceed to Castlebar, the county town, fifteen miles from Ballina. A force of 6000 eventually gathered there, armed with many pieces of artillery and well supplied with food and weapons. The British were put under the command of General Gerard Lake, the brutal, relentless victor of Vinegar Hill two months earlier. Humbert, in his marvellously impressive scarlet coat and cockade, led a total of 2000 mixed French and Irish troops out to meet Lake's forces, having left 200 of his best men to hold Killala and defend his frigates.

The British were ready for them, facing the Foxford road with artillery and men advantageously deployed. The local soldiers, however, were able to lead the republicans on a route along the west side of the extensive Lough Conn and it came as a surprise when Lake's scouts reported that the enemy were advancing but by a direct route south. Arriving outside the town at 6.00am on 27 August, the French-Irish force faced the hastily redeployed cannon. Casualties were heavy until the French officers found an area of scrub and tangled briary that gave some cover and allowed them to mount a bayonet charge that frightened the part-time militiamen, who ran away even before the French could reach their lines. With an unerring sense of self-preservation some members of the Longford and Kilkenny militias joined the rebels and began to attack the Crown forces. The regulars tried to hold the line but were quickly overcome or joined the flight. They were not pursued far beyond the town limits but continued until they reached Tuam, nearly forty miles away, in County Galway. It was said that had not Charles Cornwallis (1738-1805), Lord Lieutenant of Ireland, arrived at Athlone, the Castlebar racers would have crossed the Shannon.

It was a mighty but costly victory with more than a hundred casualties occurring during the Republicans' first charge at the artillery. It was enough, however, to encourage the republicans to set up an independent Republic of Connacht with John Moore, the Catholic son of a local merchant, as president.

BALLINAMUCK
8 SEPTEMBER 1798

The 'Races of Castlebar', an irresistible soubriquet in the circumstances, had been a decisive, if costly, victory for the republican army of Connacht and if General Jean-Joseph Humbert had followed his instructions to wait until further French reinforcements arrived the savagery of Ballinamuck might have been avoided. In fact no significant extra French were sent and like all of the 1798 enterprises Humbert's campaign was doomed to failure. Cornwallis may have been appalled at the behaviour of his soldiers and their yeoman and militia allies but they were the only men he had and General Gerard Lake, although savage, was effective. Humbert's instinct as a soldier was to act rather than wait and he hoped that by heading for Ulster he might precipitate a general rising there in spite of the failure of McCracken and Monroe. He met serious opposition at Carricknagat, near Collooney, seven miles from Sligo, on 5 September but one of the Irish officers of Humbert's regular army, Lieutenant Bartholomew Teeling, singlehandedly wiped out a gun implacement and helped Humbert to win the encounter.

The news from Ulster was discouraging so, hearing that rebellions had broken out in Longford and Westmeath, Humbert swung south to join them. He crossed Shannon at Ballintra on 7 September and there learned of the huge number of British forces ranged against him. He decided to make a stand near Ballinamuck on the Longford-Leitrim border. Cornwallis was on his right, twenty miles away at Carrick-on-Shannon. He had 15,000 men and Lake was following from the north with 14,000. When all the troops were in place the battle began with a formal blast of cannon fire followed by a charge of dragoons. When the dragoons reached the French frontline it became obvious that the engagement was a pure formality, engaged in merely to satisfy a French ideal of *honneur*. Humbert ordered his men to lay down their muskets after half an hour. This ideal of *honneur* was adhered to as far as the French soldiers were concerned, with Lake's ceremonial acceptance of Humbert's sabre. Ninety-eight French officers and 748 men were taken by canal to Dublin and later repatriated.

For some reason the terms of surrender did not seem to apply to the Irish members of Humbert's army, who were set upon by Crown infantry and dragoons. Five hundred were killed on the site and 200 taken prisoner. Most of these were hanged in Carrick-on-Shannon, including Lieutenant Teeling, although he had been a member of Humbert's regular army. Some with elements of French uniforms claimed successfully that they were part of Humbert's army. Others were transported to Botany Bay, there to begin the process that would inevitably lead to an Independent Republic of Australia. A large section of the Crown forces were given the task of extirpating any trace of the Republic of Connacht. This they did with their customary cruel efficiency, with indiscriminate burning and hanging of leaders including Father Andrew Conroy, who had led the United army through the 'Windy Gap' on the back road from Ballina to Castlebar during the night of 26-27 August. The President of the Republic, John Moore, was captured in Castlebar and died in prison. Killala, where the dream began, fell on the 23 September to the all-conquering army of General Trench: his 3000 soldiers made mincemeat of the 800 rebels and the few French left in defence of the town. His cavalry killed 400 rebels in the streets of the town.

The Year of the French had lasted barely a month.

Tory Island
12 October 1798

The last battle of the insurrection of 1798 was fought, not by Irishmen nor on Irish soil but at sea off the stormy waters of Tory Sound. (Tory Island lies seven and a half miles north-west of Horn Head in County Donegal.) The protagonists were the navy of revolutionary France and the better equipped, swifter and larger Royal Navy of Britain. The latter had with some justice praised the 'wooden wall' that had long been the British island's greatest defence. Its blockade of European ports had allowed the British to carry on the struggle with France since the start of the Revolution and the victory of Horatio Nelson (1758-1805) at Trafalgar in 1805 would save it from any chance of invasion.

France had already made several attempts to land an expeditionary force in Ireland, most notably in December 1796 in an invasion at Bantry Bay, but this attempt failed, largely defeated by weather and the British blockade. This last desperate throw had Wolfe Tone (1763-98), the only Irishman of significance in the battle, acting as gunnery officer on board the battleship *Hoche*.

The French, unaware that Humbert's daring campaign had collapsed at Ballinamuck on 8 September, sent a small fleet of eight frigates led by the *Hoche* out from Brest under the command of Commodore Jean-Baptiste-François Bompart on 16 September. Although they started the voyage in the dark they were soon spotted by a British frigate squadron led by HMS *Boadicea*. The skipper of the squadron, Richard Keats, set two of his ships, the *Ethalion* and the *Sylph*, to follow the French in hot pursuit while he rendezvoused with the rest of the Channel fleet. There followed a kind of deadly maritime game of chess, aggravated by the usual stormy weather of the north Atlantic around Tory Island. As he went with full sail up the Donegal coast, Bompart was dogged by the squadron of Sir John Borlase Warren. As a feint he ordered that the leaking *Résolue* be beached on Tory and that flares should be fired but the command was ignored. Bompart had no alternative but to attack to British fleet, hoping to force his way through.

At 7.00 on the morning of 12 October Warren ordered *Robust* to head straight for the *Roche* while the British *Magnanime* engaged the *Immortalité*, *Loire* and *Belltone*. This allowed a gap that enabled the *Ethalion*, *Melampus* and *Amelia* to close with the isolated and badly damaged *Hoche*. She had lost a topmast the day before and when the faster ships saw her condition they fired a few shells, seeing that she was drifting low in the steep Atlantic stream. As the battle continued nearly all the ships of the fleet were either sunk or captured. The *Hoche* finally surrendered at 10.50 am, with 270 of its crew killed or seriously wounded.

One prisoner was of special interest to the government authorities: Wolfe Tone, dressed in the uniform of a French colonel, had been advised by Bompart to transfer to one of the faster frigate but refused, with a sense of fatality. The prisoners were landed at Buncrana in Lough Swilly, a landlocked sea inlet, which was used as a base for the Royal Navy until the final surrender of the Treaty ports in 1938.

THE NINETEENTH CENTURY

DUBLIN
23 JULY 1803

After the Act of Union that became law on 1 January 1801, Ireland was at last quiet. Two years had passed since the cataclysm of the insurrection of 1798 that had cost 30,000 Irish lives and the surviving leaders were safely in prison in Fort St George in Scotland. Among these were Thomas Addis Emmet (1764-1827) and Thomas Russell (1767-1803), sometime librarian of the Belfast Society for Promoting Knowledge. Emmet's younger brother Robert (1778-1803) visited them in 1800 and they approved the younger man's decision to make yet another attempt to 'break in twain the galling chain and free our native land'. Myles Byrne (1780-1862), another veteran of the rebellion, offered help from Wexford, as did Michael Dwyer (1772-1825) who still roamed at large in the fastness of the Wicklow glens. There was a firm belief that if certain strategic sites in Dublin such as the Castle, the Pigeon House explosive store, the Royal Barracks in Phoenix Park and the army command post at Mary Street were successfully seized and if help arrived simultaneously from France – the old dream – a new insurrection, hard lessons learned from the past, might succeed.

When Britain's war with France was resumed on 18 May 1803 after a fifteen-month peace it seemed an appropriate time to begin to plan the new rebellion. The month of August was chosen and Emmet began to purchase arms and store them in preparation. He virtually financed his own rising. He acquired a number of properties for use as arms depots close to the Castle: in Dirty

Lane, off Thomas Street, Patrick Street, Winetavern Street and Smithfield. Byrne openly transported timber for pikes, effective weapons in street fighting since muskets took so long to reload, and for a type of exploding log invented by the ingenious Emmet, hollowed out and filled with powder. They also experimented with rockets.

This preoccupation with explosives proved to be disastrous to the plan. The chief bomb maker, a man called Johnstone, caused an accidental explosion in the Patrick Street depot on 16 July. The conspirators panicked, expecting the security forces soon to discover the extent of the plotting, and urged Emmet to bring forward the date of the rising by one week, to 23 July. They would use local workers, many of them weavers from the Coombe in the city, to make the initial strike. These were led by Jemmy Hope (1764-c. 1846), a weaver from Templepatrick who had avoided capture in Antrim. Byrne would have his '98 veterans in position at the Coal Quay, while Dwyer, who had a price on his head, insisted that he would not appear with his Wicklow outlaws unless he was certain that the Castle had been taken. Michael Quigley, another veteran of 98, had returned from France and could vouch for the men of Kildare.

On the day the men of Kildare duly arrived but were appalled by the paucity of firearms, no more than eighteen blunderbusses and six muskets. Immediately they turned for home and advised the latecomers they met along the Naas road to do the same, saying that the rising had been postponed until the following Wednesday. By now the authorities should have been alerted. One Castle spy who lived in Palmerstown reported that his employees had asked for their pay because they had to go into the city to take part in a rising. Nason Browne, a suburban innkeeper, claimed later that they heard some of his guests openly discussing their revolutionary plans.

In the heart of the city chaos reigned: copies of the proclamation of the republic had arrived but not the high ladders necessary for scaling the rear walls of the Castle. No one had thought to bring the detonators for Emmet's patent exploding logs. The six empty coaches that were intended to take the assailants and their weapons into the Castle were stopped on their way to the Thomas Street depot by a mounted soldier who asked them their purpose. He was shot by Ned Conlon, one of Emmet's men, acting as outrider, and at once the drivers turned and fled the scene.

It was a typical Saturday night in Dublin with crowded streets and drunken revellers. The revellers seized an abundance of newly fashioned pikes lying about Temple Bar and soon they had turned into a uncontrollable mob that roamed the narrow streets with no fixed purpose. By sheer ill luck the coach of Lord Kilwarden, the unusually humane Lord Chief Justice, was surrounded and he and his nephew, the Reverend Richard Wolfe, were piked to death. In all fifty people were killed wantonly in similar fashion.

Believing a false report that the army was on the streets Emmet decided to die fighting. He swiftly donned his self-designed uniform of white breeches, green coat with gold epaulettes and abundantly plumed hat and with a few faithful companions sallied forth to meet the opposition. But there was none to meet. Byrne's forces had not seen the rocket that was to have been their signal to take action, and quietly left the scene. Emmet and his followers headed for their headquarters in Rathfarnham, leaving the murderous riot to run its course. The last ambitious rising had turned into a bloody shambles around Thomas Street, where Emmet would make his last public appearance – on the hastily built scaffold in front of St Catherine's Church.

BALLYEAGH STRAND: A FACTION FIGHT
24 JUNE 1839

This greatest and bloodiest of the faction fights that were such a feature of life in Ireland in the early part of the nineteenth century took place on Ballyeagh Strand near Ballybunion, County Kerry, in the summer of 1839. Long regarded as recreational violence, some of these fights now seem to have had elements of sectarian conflict, such as is still characteristic of the soccer clashes between the supporters of Rangers and Celtic in Glasgow and between Manchester United and Manchester City. A notable example of a continuing religious conflict was that between the 'Liberty Boys' and the 'Ormond Boys' in eighteenth-century Dublin. The Protestant tailors of the Liberties regularly engaged in bloody battles with the Catholic butchers of Ormond Market. The bridges and quays became the scene of dangerous confrontations, with leg tendons severed and butchers left hanging on their own meat hooks. In the nineteenth century faction fights were also an indication of an unspecific sense of frustration felt by a people long treated as an underclass.

Outside the city the usual scenes for faction confrontation were fairs and 'patterns'. This word came from *pátrún*, an Irish word meaning 'patron', and by association a celebration of the social rather than the religious aspects of the feast days of Irish saints, the Blessed Virgin and St John. There were also strong residual elements of not very deeply buried paganism.

The most famous of the long-lasting feuds was that between the Caravats (*carbhait*='cravats', that is to say 'nooses') and

Shanavests (*sean-veisteanna*=old vests') that flourished in the years 1806-11. It had a class basis, the Shanavests being small landowners while their adversaries were farm labourers. Their battlegrounds ranged all over the southern counties of Tipperary, Waterford, Kilkenny, Limerick and Cork. Whether sectarian or social in their origin, by the third decade of the nineteenth century fights between these factions had become a regular feature of many gatherings. By the 1820s the practice had reached such a level of violence (even if periodic) that a select committee of the House of Lords began an investigation on 18 May 1824.

The battle of Ballyeagh Strand was among the last of the fights, the reputation of which persisted long after the influence of the Church and the effective new police force established in 1836 as the Irish Constabulary slowly brought an end to them. The tradition of the 'fighting Irish' had left a dubious legacy at home and was carried across the Irish Sea and the Atlantic as the Famine years caused an explosion in emigration. So firmly had the reputation for fighting and drinking been established that the song 'Mush. Mush' with its quarrelsome couplet: 'If you're in for a row or a ruction/Jist thread on the tail o' me coat' was printed in the *Scottish Students Songbook* (1897). The theme of this pointless breaking of heads figured as one of the *Traits and Stories of the Irish Peasantry* (1830) by William Carleton (1704-1869). In it he describes how in a fight between the O'Hallaghans and the O'Callaghans, the former short of weapons and driven into a graveyard, 'furnished themselves with the best they could find, videlicet, the skull, leg, thigh and arm bones, which they found lying about the graveyard.'

Ballyeagh Strand is a beach at the mouth of the River Cashen in County Kerry just south of Ballybunion and about nine miles north-west of Listowel. The name Cashen may come from the Irish word *casán* (pathway) because the river could be forded at low tide. The feast of St John the Baptist, 24 June, was the day of the Ballyeagh Races, held, as it was customary, on the beach. About 2500 people, some from the Cooleen faction and some from the Lawlor-Blacks Mulvihils, engaged in a shillelagh fight on the seashore. The Cooleen group hailed from south of Listowel on the Tralee side while their ancient enemy came from the north side of the river. Shillelaghs were stout cudgels hewn from oak or the harder blackthorn. (The connection with the County Wicklow village of that name is at best tenuous.) The main participants were men but it was not unknown for women to take part, using the fist-sized rounded stones feely available on the seashore.

The 1200 fighters from Cooleen seemed to have gained an earlier advantage, pushing the Lawlor-Blacks Mulvihils across the river and south towards Ballyduff. An hour later, at three o'clock, a reinforced crew began to force the Cooleen faction back across the Cashen. The tide was filling rapidly and a number of them crowded on to a boat. This was immediately attacked by the Lawlor-Blacks Mulvihils, many of them on horseback. Reports of casualties from the mêlée were greatly exaggerated, rumours putting the number dead at 200. The examination of the scene by the new constabulary, however, established the death toll at fifteen with two missing but there were not surprisingly more than 200 injuries. Most of the deaths were caused by drowning in the Chasen, since none of those involved had learned to swim.

The potato blight of the next decade changed Ireland utterly and faction fights, like so many of the older ways, became a part of an unforgotten past. However it took a long time for the practice and its causes to die out completely. The county most associated with faction fighting was Tipperary and it is appropriate that the last recorded mêlée was at the fair at Cappawhite, eight miles north of Tipperary Town, in 1887.

WIDOW MCCORMACK'S CABBAGE PATCH, BALLINGARRY, COUNTY TIPPERARY 29 JULY 1848

In 1848 the young men of Young Ireland, no longer feeling the need for restraint since the great constitutionalist Daniel O'Connell (1775-1847) had died, fell victim to the heady inspiration of the 'year of revolutions' in Europe that affected the capital cities of Berlin, Budapest, Prague, Rome, Vienna but most of all Paris, where the Second Republic was proclaimed. The replacement of absolutist regimes with libertarian administrations seemed to William Smith O'Brien (1803-1864), self-styled 'middle-aged' Young Irelander, the ideal solution for Ireland. He and his close colleague, Thomas Francis Meagher (1823-67) had gone to Paris to congratulate the founders of the republic and returned with a new flag for a new Ireland, modelled on the French tricolour but aimed at reconciling green and orange.

O'Brien, who claimed descent from Brian Boru, hoped that an Irish republic could be achieved with as little bloodshed as the French, and persuaded Meagher, John Blake Dillon (1816-66) and other militants including Terence Bellew MacManus (1823-60), Michael Doheny (1805-63) and James Stephens (1824-1901) – who would later claim the credit for founding the Fenian Brotherhood – to prepare for an autumn rising. John Mitchel (1815-75), the most extreme of them all, had already been sentenced for treason felony and was a convict in Tasmania. The country was riddled with government spies and the suspension of *habeas corpus* on 22 July meant that the authorities could imprison anyone they wished without trial. O'Brien decided to bring the date forward and from 23 to 29 July tried to gather support for a rising in Dublin, Wexford, Kilkenny and Tipperary.

The decade of the Great Famine was an inappropriate time to start a rebellion. Dillon received no encouragement in the capital and after a rally at Killenaule, a village in County Tipperary that should have been the beginning of the insurrection, most of the parties seemed to lose heart and headed home.

The reluctant O'Brien, described by some observers as being in a sort of dream, decided to make a stand at Ballingarry, a village seven miles to the east of Killenaule, close to the border with County Kilkenny. He had heard that a party of forty-six RIC officers, led by Sub-Inspector Trant, was making its way from Callan, eight miles away in County Kilkenny, to arrest him. Another rumour had it that a larger force of police was coming from Thurles, fifteen miles to the west. When Trant's party saw the barricades that O'Brien's followers had drawn across the road and the large crowd of mainly sightseers that clustered round them they veered right and took refuge in the large two-storey house at Farrinrory about a mile to the north of Ballingarry. It was said that as they marched in they were singing 'The British Grenadiers', apparently unaware of the irony of claiming that: 'Of all the world's great heroes there's none than can compare...'

The house belonged to Margaret McCormack, a widow, who was absent from home at the time. Her five children were taken as hostages and the house was made ready for defence, by means that included breaking up the furniture. The police pointed their guns from the windows while the disorganised rebel rabble surrounded the house. Mrs McCormack arrived and pleaded with Trant to let her children go, a request that he refused. She came across O'Brien in one of the outhouses and demanded shrilly what he intended to do about her children and her house. Together they went up to the parlour window to negotiate. He climbed on to the sill of one of the downstairs rooms and urged the occupying party to give up their arms: 'We are all Irishmen; give up your guns and you are free to go,' he said, and began to shake hands with the constable nearest him. There was some delay until Trant was fetched down from an upstairs room but he, a little hysterical at the situation in which he found himself, would not parley: 'We would forfeit our lives rather than give up our arms.' O'Brien offered them five minutes for consideration and turned away.

A shot rang out from the house, intended, it was believed, to hit O'Brien as he returned to his motley band of insurgents. Someone in the crowd replied with: 'Slash away, boys, and slaughter the whole of them.' A volley of shots from the RIC was answered and O'Brien had to be dragged out of range by Stephens and MacManus, both of whom were wounded. In the general exchange of shots one man, Thomas Walsh, was killed, as the press of the crowd pushed him from one side of the open gate to the other. Another man, Patrick McBride, safe in a crowd round the gable end of the house, found himself alone when his companions disappeared and was shot dead while trying to leap over the wall to join them. The shooting continued for some time but it soon became clear that the stout house filled with well-armed trained paramilitaries was virtually impregnable. A local priest, Philip Fitzgerald, risked his life trying to establish a ceasefire. Still O'Brien's men continued firing, although by now they were running low in ammunition. It was not until a detachment of reinforcements from Cashel barracks led by Sub-Inspector Cox came with arms blazing that the crowd began to disperse and the McCormack children were returned to their relieved mother.

O'Brien remained at large for a week until in a citizen's arrest he was apprehended at Thurles station by a railway guard who happened to be English as he tried to make his way back to his Limerick home. He was sentenced to be hanged, drawn and quartered, a savage sentence that included evisceration. In his fey way he refused to ask for a pardon. A special act of parliament had to be passed to allow the government to transport him to Tasmania with MacManus and Meagher to join Mitchel. The others eventually escaped but he was unyielding in his self-sacrifice and lived a solitary life in a cottage on an island off the

Tasmanian coast. Eventually he accepted the parole conditions and was released in a general pardon in 1854. He took no active part in politics but continued to hold out for a constitutionally obtained freedom for Ireland, writing endlessly to *The Times* about Ireland's woes until his death at the age of sixty-one.

A lasting tribute to O'Brien, to his courage and to his unflinching dignity, however miscast he may have been as a rebel leader, may be found in his O'Connell Street statue, fifth down from Parnell Square.

DOLLY'S BRAE
12 JULY 1849

The Orange Order had been banned several times since its naïve foundation at the Diamond near Loughgall in County Armagh on 21 September 1795. It also suffered from an occasional drop in interest in membership as the years went by but any show of nationalist resurgence was the occasion of revival and fresh recruitment. Sectarian tensions had lessened a little during 'Black '47' but the Young Ireland Rising of 1848 stirred atavistic feelings again. The Twelfth of July celebrations of the Battle of the Boyne that year had all the noise and venom of older days, and the government sent troops to prevent any serious outbreak of civil disorder.

There was, however, trouble in mid-Down at a tiny Catholic village built on a hill called Dolly's Brae, near Castlewellan, four miles from Newcastle. A continuing characteristic of the Orange Order is the arrogation of the right to walk 'anywhere on the Queen's highway', however incendiary the action. On their way to the 'field' at Rathfriland (also 'on the hill', as the song describes it) ten miles west of Castlewellan, Orangemen chose to march, for the first time, through Dolly's Brae. A serious uprising did not occur in the nineteenth century apart from Robert Emmet's Saturday night débacle in 1803 and the farce of the Widow MacCormack's cabbage patch in 1848. There were, however, many examples of outrages by secret societies, especially during the 'Tithe Wars' that peaked in the 1830s: in Ulster a group known as Ribbonmen carried on a Defenderist tradition, seeing themselves as the

Catholics' only defence against the wilder excesses of Orangeism.

On 12 July 1849 there was no trouble on the outward journey, even although the obviously armed Orangemen sang anti-Catholic songs as they marched through the hamlet. On their way home Robert Jocelyn, 3rd Earl of Roden, (1788-1870), a known bigot, entertained them and other lodgers rather too well at his Tollymore demesne and urged them to 'do their duty as loyal Protestants'. He also ordered the dragoons sent to monitor the situation to escort them home to Newcastle. In spite of advice from the escorts the Orangemen insisted on marching back through Dolly's Brae but 500 Catholics including some Ribbonmen confronted them at Magheramayo, armed with muskets and pikes. A first shot was fired, probably by an Orangeman, although it was afterwards said to have been fired by a Catholic. In the battle that followed thirty Catholics were killed, mainly from the village, some burned to death inside their houses. The only good result of the unequal confrontation was the passing of the Party Processions Act of 1850, which was intended to outlaw provocative marches and meetings. In fact the act was ignored and magistrates were too partial or spineless to enforce it.Roden was censured and removed from the magistracy.

Dolly's Brae has remained an important item on the Orange blazon and several ballads have been written about the paltry event, one including the line: 'We'll kick the Pope all over Dolly's Brae'. A more printable one ends with the stanza:

> Come all ye blind-led papists, wherever that ye be,
> Never bow down to priest or Pope, for them they will disown.
> Never bow down to images, for God ye must adore.
> Come, join our Orange heroes and cry 'Dolly's Brae' no more.

EASTER WEEK, APRIL 1916

Mount Street Bridge
26 April 1916

There were few pitched battles during the Easter Rising: the rebellion consisted largely of occupation of certain buildings and holding on grimly until a necessary and reluctant surrender. There were, however, two incidents that qualify for the title of battle: Mount Street Bridge and Ashbourne. Mount Street Bridge is at the end of Northumberland Road, where the road crosses over the Grand Canal. It runs south-east from Merrion Square and is crossed at the bridge by Haddington Road coming from the south-west.

The participants in the battle were a column of Sherwood Foresters en route to the city centre from Kingstown and some of the rebel riflemen from Boland's Bakery based in houses close to the bridge – two in Haddington Road, three in 25 Northumberland Road and seven in Clanwilliam House on Mount Street.

Boland's bakery, located in Grand Canal Street, was the battle centre for the 3rd Battalion of volunteers under the command of Éamon de Valera (1882-1975). The outposts were ideally placed for doing maximum damage to the Tommies as they crowded over the bridge. Most of the soldiers were little more than boys so naïve that they thought they had been landed in France and were amazed that the French natives could speak English so well. They had been in uniform for a mere eight weeks and many had never even fired a rifle. They had joined up as part of the deadly 'pals' recruiting drive of the First World War that resulted in all the young men of whole streets, factory workshops and villages joining up together and dying together.

The 178th brigade from the North Midlands arrived late on the Tuesday evening of Easter week and were greeted by flag-waving crowds, elated that their saviours had come to put an end to the unpopular rebellion. Coming from Nottingham and with the name of Sherwood Foresters it was inevitable that they would become known as the 'Robin Hoods'. The brigade was divided into two battalions: one half approached the city along Stillorgan Road and reached Kingsbridge Station and Kilmainham without opposition. The other half, the 2/7th and 2/8th battalions, came in by Merrion Road, a route that would lead them through Ballsbridge and the bridge over the canal. The day was fine and the Robin Hoods marched steadily on without helmets and in some cases without appropriate ammunition.

Among the jubilant crowds of cheering, tea-serving civilians were the wife and children of Captain Frederick Dietrichsen of the sherwood foresters, who had been sent by him to the safety of his mother-in-law's house in Blackrock, to avoid the Zeppelin raids at home in England. He was able to speak to them briefly, unaware of the battle ahead, of which he would be one of the first casualties. When the soldiers reached the end of Northumberland Road, Michael Malone and James Grace, both expert marksmen opened fire from number 25: ten Robin Hoods fell at this first volley. The soldiers in columns four abreast continued to advance, led by officers who because of their position had drawn sabres and were moving to attack the house. The Volunteers were able to make the bridge a killing ground. Fire was experienced literally left, right and centre.

The first shots were fired at exactly 12.25 and the battle lasted until seven o'clock that evening, when the insurgent posts were cleared and set on fire. The casualty list among the British included four officers – as well as fourteen wounded – and 216 other ranks were killed, among the Sherwoods. There were four dead among the Volunteers. These included Malone, de Valera's most trusted and effective lieutenant, and three of those who had positioned themselves in Clanwilliam House. Number 25 Northumberland still has a plaque dedicated to Malone. Grace survived only to be captured the following day. He was discovered by the owner hiding in an outhouse in Haddington Road and he informed the army.

It was a notable propaganda boost for the Volunteers but showed the army leader Brigadier William Lowe (1861-c. 1940) up as a poor tactician. Against all the advice of his officers at the site he insisted upon that the bridge be taken by bayonet, if necessary. He must have been aware that Leeson Street Bridge, two-thirds of a mile away, was virtually undefended and could have been used for side and rear enfilades that would have ended the action much earlier. As it was the growing pile of dead bodies was used as a kind of rampart by their comrades, who were relentlessly ordered to advance, against all reason. One of the stories of the time was that fire from the motley collection of Volunteer guns was so fierce that the barrels had to be cooled by sardine oil saved from their front-line rations. And in Clanwilliam House before hand grenades reached the gas supply and set the place on fire, a dressmaker's model was clad in Volunteer uniform and placed in a window, where it was shot to pieces by the Robin Hoods.

Recent research has suggested that there were odd tactical decisions made on both sides. A greater knowledge of the local topography on the part of the Robin Hoods's officers could have saved soldiers' lives. There were many ways that Clanwilliam House could have been attacked from the rear by sending troops from St Mary's Road down Haddington Lane and across Haddington Road. The few Volunteers who caused such havoc could and should have been relieved by any of the 120 men who were at ease in Boland's Mill. But then historians are always wiser than the participants.

Ashbourne, County Meath
27 April 1916

The Easter Rising, although intended to be countrywide, was almost totally confined to Dublin city centre. One action, however, an unusually successful one, occurred fifteen miles north of the capital on the N2 road to Slane. One mile north of the village of Ashbourne, County Meath, is the Rath crossroads. It was here that the Dublin Brigade's 5th ('Fingal') battalion of Volunteers had a significant victory. The commandant oratorially and emotionally was Thomas Ashe (1885-1917) but Richard Mulcahy (1886-1971), later second-in-command to Michael Collins (1890-1922), was the tactician. Ashe, a Kerryman, was the principal of Lusk NS nine miles to the east; Mulcahy, who was born in Waterford and worked as a post-office clerk. Ashe responded with great fervour and feeling to every word from the mouth of Pearse but did not always have the tactical nous to implement his wishes.

The Fingal brigade's purpose was the generally harrying of government installations and personnel in the countryside around north County Dublin. On Easter Monday, the day the GPO and other important buildings were occupied and the Proclamation of the Irish Republic was read, sixty Volunteers appeared for duty, half the number of the muster of the day before. Considering the area they had to cover the 5th battalion was fairly mobile; there was only one private car, a two-seater Morris, but all the Monday Volunteers had bicycles. Ashe, on orders from Pearse, told one of his men to blow up the Great Northern Railway viaduct at Rogerstown but would not allow him to wait until low tide. (The result was near failure because of the difficulty of attaching the dynamite to the pillars at the flood.) On the Wednesday they attacked the barracks of the Royal Irish Constabulary (RIC) in Swords and smashed the telegraph instruments in the Post Office. The police obligingly surrendered five carbines, the only weapons they had. It meant that Fingal, as a fighting unit, continued to be seriously underarmed, holding at most a few dozen rifles and a dozen single-shot carbines.

Ashe reluctantly tried to accede to another urgent request from Pearse for forty men to add to the numbers in the GPO, but he could afford to send only twenty. This left just forty Volunteers under his command but as with so much else about his operations it proved to be an advantage. Without fully realising it Mulcahy and he were already devising the methods of guerrilla warfare and the use of what were not yet called 'flying columns' that would be such a feature of the 'Tan' War Later on the day of the disappointing Swords raid one of the columns managed to commandeer a Kennedy's Bakery van full of bread, solving the commissariat problems and doubling the brigade's motorised transport capacity. Although still ill-equipped, the brigade's leaders readily agreed to the latest orders from the GPO that arrived on Friday morning: they were to cut the railway track at Batterstown, twelve miles due west of Swords, and on the way to attack the RIC barracks at Ashbourne. They ran into a frail barricade manned by two RIC constables at Rath Cross. These were easily captured and the constables marched down by a Volunteer party to the barracks in the village to accept their surrender.

The rest of the Volunteers were engaged in having the barricade removed when it became clear that a motorised party of fifty-five men in seventeen cars was speeding along the road from Slane. The volunteers later realised that the party was led by a chief inspector. The leading vehicle was a mere 200 yards from the column before the rebels noticed it. Ashe's reaction was to withdraw in the face of a much superior force but Mulcahy, with his instinctive sense of tactics, persuaded him to attack from the rear, having pinned down the advance guard with accurate fire. It was in essence an improvised ambush and took the RIC party completely by surprise. Mulcahy sent two groups of Volunteers to attack from north and south. At one stage they were so successful that during an increase of fire each assumed that reinforcements had arrived. The terrain, which was flat, with high-banked ditches, suited the quasi-ambush but it was only afterwards that the Volunteers realised that their two groups had been shooting at each other. The reluctance of the RIC party to engage with people they knew as their fellow countrymen contributed greatly to the Fingal success in the fighting. RIC leader, County Inspector Gray, was wounded early in the fight, dying of his wounds a fortnight later, and DI Smith, his second-in-command, was killed at the scene.

The RIC party, with greater manpower and armaments, could easily have overcome their attackers had they charged. Instead they halted the convoy, thereby giving the flanking parties easier targets. Soon, essentially leaderless, the policemen walked quietly down to the main road to surrender, while those in the Ashbourne barracks, who had taken no part in the fighting except to withdraw their previous offer of surrender, also marched to the crosswords. The fighting had lasted five hours. Two of Ashe's men had been killed and five wounded, while on the RIC side eight had died and fifteen had been wounded. The Battle of Ashbourne, although none realised it at the time, had given a template for the coming struggle.

Thomas Ashe died from force-feeding while on hunger strike in Mountjoy Jail in September 1917.

THE WAR OF INDEPENDENCE 1920-1

BALLINALEE, COUNTY LONGFORD
4 NOVEMBER 1920

The battle of Ballinalee was fought by the North Longford Flying Column against superior British forces in November 1920. The leader of the column was Seán Mac Eoin, a well-known blacksmith and farmer from the district. Born John Joseph McKeon on 30 September 1893, he began using the Irish version of his name in 1904 and was only a month from his twenty-seventh birthday when the battle that made him famous took place. In October orders came from Dublin that two officers of the RIC stationed in Granard, Captain Philip St John Kelleher, a much-decorated officer from the 4th Leinster Regiment and a District-Inspector in the RIC, and his assistant, Constable Peter Cooney officially were, targets. When they were shot on 31 October and 1 November respectively the reaction of Crown forces was expectedly severe. Most of the inhabitants of Mac Eoin's village of Ballinalee decided to abandon their homes. They could see from a dull red glow in the distance that the Crown forces had set the town of Granard alight and feared that their village, eight miles away, would be next.

Mac Eoin assumed that the attack would come from the Granard direction and drew up his defence plan on that understanding; he posted Seán Duffy with a detachment at the schoolhouse on the Granard Road, Frank Davis on the road from Ballinamuck, with Hugh Hourican at the Protestant church guarding the Longford road to the south-west. Mac Eoin stayed at the village crossroads with his brother Jimmy, Seamus Conway,

Sean Sexton and Tommy Early. Each of the outposts was under strict instructions not to begin firing until Mac Eoin gave the signal.

Then began the long dark rainy wait that ended dramatically at 1 am on 4 November. Up to eleven military trucks with blazing headlights appeared on the Granard road. The battle began with two grenades thrown at the leading lorry and rapid rifle fire from all Mac Eoin's outposts. This was answered by British machine-gun fire that echoed eerily through the deserted village. The shooting took place in complete darkness so the Tommies often turned out to be shooting at their own men.

After about an hour of indeterminate shooting Mac Eoin, with unbelievable chutzpah, called on the British to surrender and was even more surprised when they in turn asked for conditions. His ambitious demand for unconditional surrender was met, after a period of consultation, with the surprising question: 'What if we don't surrender?' Mac Eoin replied, 'Then it's a fight to the finish' and with those words the intensity of the confrontation decreased. There was a noise of engines being started, gears crashed into reverse and a slow withdrawal of the army trucks. In subsequent army reports the number of rebels was estimated at 500, judged, presumably, by the intensity of the returned fire. This caused a deal of amusement among the 'five hundred', none of whom had received the merest scratch. The engagement passed into history as a mighty victory and Mac Eoin was given the Homeric title, 'Blacksmith of Ballinalee'. He had many further battles before the long war was over, collecting a death sentence and after the treaty of 1920 generalship in the Free State army in which he had to fight against old comrades. Later he had a career in politics.

KILMICHAEL
28 NOVEMBER 1920

Kilmichael is a village in west Cork about nine miles from Macroom on the road to Dunmanway. It was near here that a bloody and successful ambush of 'Auxies' took place on Sunday 28 November 1920. It was laid by the West Cork Flying Column commanded by Tom Barry (1897-1980) who wrote an account of the incident in his book *Guerrilla Days in Ireland* (1949) that was later challenged by several historians. Whatever about such details, it was the most successful action ever against the detested 'Auxies'. The squad of the Auxliary Royal Irish Constabulary had been first commissioned in July 1920, intended as an officer echelon for the beleaguered RIC. All the members were commissioned officers and in practice acted independently of both the old RIC and the 'Black and Tans'. The force quickly earned a reputation for drunkenness, brutality and uncontrollability that caused their commander Brigadier General Frank Crozier (1879-1937) to resign in February 1921. Auxies had a reputation for steely reprisals and had been involved in the notorious 'Bloody Sunday' events in Dublin on 21 November, a week earlier.

The cadets, as they were known, commanded by DI Francis Crake and travelling in two Crossley tenders, were on their usual triangular patrol route: Macroom, Dunmanway, Bandon and back to Macroom. Crossleys were sturdy vehicles but being open apart from the cab were rather uncomfortable in the prevailing wet winter weather of County Cork. The Auxies's route was a much travelled one especially in the winter, and pub gossip and the watchful eyes of the local people could give a tolerably accurate estimate of its timing. Tom Barry had served in the British army at Ypres and Mesopotamia in the Great War and his military experience was obvious in the planning and execution of the ambush that took place in the townland of Shanacashel between 4.05 and 4.20 on a twilit, windy afternoon.

The operation began at 8.15am at the chosen site, a little south of Kilmachael, on the road to Dunmanway. Barry had thirty-six men under his command, most of them unused to action of any sort but as he advised them of his plan he made it clear that it was to be one of the most significant actions of the War of Independence. He made good use of the terrain, which had stone walls and rocky bluffs and followed a sharp bend in the road. The command position was behind a low wall that faced the road that the Auxies were expected to use. Forty yards further along the road was a large erratic ten feet high that gave an excellent view of the road and the command post; he stationed his first section there. Another outcrop about 150 yards from the first was held by Barry's second group, while the third occupied positions behind rocks. A fourth party was positioned at a distance along the road to deal with a possible third tender. All the Volunteers were in their places by 9am and the long wait began.

Just after 4pm Barry's scouts on the Macroom side of Kil-michael reported the approach of the expected tenders and word was sent from the command post to the other groups. Just before the Auxies arrived a horse and trap carrying five armed IRA volunteers came along the road and had to be quickly sidelined to a by-road. As the first Crossley turned the corner it was flagged down by what looked like a man in the uniform of a British officer. As the vehicle slowed down and almost stopped a Mills bomb was thrown from the command post, killing the driver and his front–seat passenger. The rest of the column opened fire, killing nine of the Auxies, while those in the command post, running low behind the wall, fired on the second tender. Seventeen combatants in all were killed, including DI Crake, with three fatalities on Barry's side: Michael McCarthy, Jim Sullivan and Pat Deasy. Barry, in a shrewd psychological move did not praise his battle-shocked men but berated them as near failures, making them march through the carnage of the dead and the still burning tenders. Then he ordered that all weapons be removed from the corpses to add to his own depleted store and gathered any documentation that the dead soldiers carried in their pockets. Not long after 4.30 the column was on the move again south and by 11pm it had crossed the River Bandon at Granure. There the men spent the night in an empty cottage. Next day they were tended by the Ballyinacarriga IRA, who provided food, shelter and much–needed rest.

The Kilmichael ambush has been the source of much division among commentators. Some argue that after Bloody Sunday Lloyd George was being forced by world opinion to move with characteristic slowness towards the concept of a truce and that Kilmichael stopped this progress. Others say that it was the brutal efficiency that made him realise that he did not have 'murder by the throat', as he often boasted and that the Tan War could not be won by the Black and Tans, the Auxies and the army. The other source of historiological disagreement is the question of the Auxies 'false' surrender. Barry's given reason for the merciless killing of the occupants of the second tender was that they offered to surrender and then killed two IRA men who approached them. General Crozier in his book *Ireland Forever* (1932) – incidentally remarkably favourable towards the Irish cause – states that one of the 'surrendered' Auxies did shoot two of Barry's fatalities and that the slaughter that followed, if disproportionate, was only to be expected in the circumstances. Barry's command: 'Keep firing and don't stop until I tell ye,' was carried out to the letter. Other charges made against Barry's men was that the bodies of the dead Auxies were mutilated with axes but this charge was replaced by the lesser one that post-mortem wounds were inflicted by bayonets or revolvers.

The Auxies were feared particularly for the indiscriminate and violent nature of their reprisals. This took the form of torture of prisoners, shooting on sight and in this case joining with a party of Tans as drunken as themselves to set fire to the centre of Cork city on 11 December. They prevented the city fire services from reaching the sites of many of the conflagrations and looted what they could from the burning. A report by General Strickland, the Cork OC, could not be published because its effect 'would be disastrous for the government's whole policy in Ireland'. Three million pounds (at least £120m today) was later paid in compensation.

So effective and shocking an episode was bound to be applauded and execrated with equal intensity. The name of Kilmichael became known around the world. At home the balladeers did not neglect the opportunity of celebrating it. The chorus of 'The Boys of Kilmichael' more than adequately sums up the contemporary nationalist view:

> *O forget not the boys of Kilmichael,*
> *Those brave boys both gallant and true.*
> *They fought with Tom Barry's bold column*
> *And conquered the red, white and blue.*

CLONMULT
20 FEBRUARY 1921

Clonmult is a village about seven miles north of Midleton in south-east County Cork. A disused farmhouse in a sheltered place overlooking it was chosen as assembly post by the 4th Battalion of the 1st Cork Brigade, who were planning to ambush a troop train at Cobh Junction, expected there on 22 February. The unit was commanded by Commandant Diarmuid O'Hurley, with Vice-Commandant Joseph Aherne as second-in-command. These two, along with Captain Patrick Whelan, left the house to reconnoitre the target area and consider the arrangements they should make for the success of the attack. They sought a suitable place at Dooneen to which the volunteers could be transferred. Captain Jack O'Connell was left as acting officer-in-charge. Of the unit of twenty-two volunteers, nine, including Joseph Aherne, were from Midleton, with five others from Cobh. O'Hurley was from the Bandon unit.

On the morning of Sunday 20 February Michael Desmond and John Joe Joyce, two of the volunteers from Midleton, left the building to fetch water from a nearby spring. They had not gone far before they noticed unmistakable signs that the farmhouse was being surrounded by British forces. They ran back to the house to warn the rest, firing as they went, but both were killed. The noise of the shooting sufficiently alarmed their companions inside. A number of these, including Captain James Aherne from Cobh and Michael Hallahan from Midleton, were killed as they tried to break out of the closing circle and reach Midleton to get help from the small local company. Aherne almost succeeded in clearing a fence 200 yards from the hideout. The acting OC, Jack O'Connell, did succeed in reaching safety but there was little he could do on a Sunday to get help.

The army were close enough to set the farmhouse on fire and some soldiers to without success widen a gap in the gable end When the defenders tried to surrender by appearing with hands aloft at the doorway six were killed in a burst of fire from a party of Black and Tans who had come to reinforce the army. The rest were taken prisoner; of these two, Paddy O'Sullivan and Maurice Moore, were executed at Cork military barracks on 28 April, five others had their death sentences commuted and one, Captain Paddy Higgins, who had been wounded in the mouth, was saved from execution by the Truce, which came into effect on 11 July.

It was unusual for such a complete defeat of the IRA to have happened. Was security at the farmhouse lax? For once, could the enemy's intelligence have been more effective than the IRA's? Throughout the War of Independence the Crown forces' sources of information, especially in the south-west, could not match that of the various flying columns. At times the combined forces of army, RIC, Black and Tans and Auxiliaries, felt that not just the men of the IRA units but the whole of, in this case, Munster were ranged against them. Something unusual had happened at Clonmult. Had pub conversation, the usual source of good product, tempted someone to inform? Was the mission of O'Hurley (who was killed on 28 May in another affray) not as secret as he had hoped? Nationalist history much prefers to dwell on the victories over the Crown forces, such as Kilmichael and Crossbarry. The story of clonmult did not appear in any nationalist history book.

CROSSBARRY
19 MARCH 1921

After their success at Kilmichael, Barry's flying column continued their part on the Tan War with increasing effect. Their next 'spectacular' was the Crossbarry ambush when he and Liam Deasy (1898-1974) engaged with the soldiers of the Essex regiment at the village twelve miles south-west of Cork city on a side road to Bandon. Before the engagement a number of volunteers were arrested after the failed ambush of a troop train at Upton Junction, near Crossbarry, on 15 February 1921. One of the IRA men broke under torture and revealed that the headquarters of the successful West Cork Brigade were in Ballymurphy and that Barry's column had returned to the area after a frustrated attempt at an ambush on St Patrick's Day at Ship pool on the Kinsale-Bandon road. Realising that Barry's men were waiting, the targets withdrew and returned to Kinsale.

A major military operation was immediately set up, involving 1200 soldiers drawn from all over County Cork. 120 Auxies from Bandon were also mobilised. This assembly was in position by the evening of 18 March. Crown forces effectively encircled Crossbarry and began to close the net very early on the morning of 19 March. Barry, not realising the extent of the forces involved, intended to use his usual ambush tactics, with two mines laid on the roadway and his band of 104 volunteers divided into six attack groups and one as a rearguard. At 6.30am the military had an early success, surprising Charlie Hurley, one of the IRA commanders, in what had been a safe house in Ballymurphy. He was killed as he attempted to fight his way out. Word reached Barry of the extent and disposition of the Crown forces and he realised that he and his men would have to fight their way to safety. Each of his men had about forty rounds and Barry decided that a rearguard action was impossible. He reckoned that if the main force could be broken down into smaller units he might succeed in breaking out of the trap.

One unit of the British forces had advanced towards Crossbarry and seemed to be of a size that Barry's men could attempt to defeat. This crucial unit of about twelve vehicles drove straight into crossfire from as close as ten yards away. They very wisely retreated after such heavy fire. However six soldiers and one RIC constable died and their weaponry was collected and the lorries set on fire. When the Crown forces began to realise what had happened they began to move towards the scene of the ambush. A column of 100 men when the Crown forces attacked the ambush position from the south-west but they too met stiff opposition. In the confusion Barry moved his men to the safety of Gurranereigh.

Major Percival of the Essex Regiment tried to engage the IRA with long-range fire but without success. Later he blamed the Auxie column for leaving a gap in the encirclement. The combined Crown forces of 1200 serving soldiers and 120 Auxies had thus been unable to defeat Barry's 104 Volunteers. Inevitably there were different estimates of casualties. Apart from the six soldiers and one RIC constable, Arthur Frederick Kenward, who were killed during the first engagement, there were at least twenty casualties on the British side, compared with fewer than six of Barry's men.

HEADFORD JUNCTION
21 MARCH 1921

In March 1921 a column of the Kerry No 2 Brigade received intelligence that a party of thirty soldiers of the 1st Battalion of the Royal Fusiliers were travelling by train from Kenmare to Killarney after picking up supplies of food. The troops would have to change trains from the branch line to the main line at Headford Junction and wait there for fifty minutes. An ambush was set up at Headford on Sunday 20 March 1921 with the purpose of obtaining supplies of weapons. This engagement proved to be the biggest and bloodiest battle in Kerry during the Tan War. The column was under the command of Dan Allman, with Tom McEllistrim as second-in-command.

The column consisted of thirty-two local volunteers. Ten of these were positioned on the Mallow side of the junction, while the rest found what cover they could in the railway buildings, commandeering the stationmaster's house but allowing the family to leave. These preparations were interrupted by the arrival of the Kenmare train ten minutes early. Three of the leaders, Allman, Johnny O'Connor and Dan Healy, were still in the middle of the platform and had to race for the nearest cover, the station lavatory. Some others took up positions on an embankment overlooking the station. The troops, under the command of Lieutenant C.F. Adams, began to dismount to await the Tralee train and one soldier ran straight into the lavatory, to be confronted by the armed Volunteers, who tried to disarm him. Instinctively he tried to use his rifle and was shot by Allman.

A general exchange of fire followed and Lieutenant Adams was one of the early victims, shot through the chest. The civilians who had alighted were mainly cattle and pig dealers and were caught in crossfire. John Breen and Patrick O'Donoghue from Killarney and Michael Cagney from Liscarroll were early casualties. Timothy McCarthy, a merchant from Loo Bridge, twelve miles from Killarney, tried to protect his three-year-old daughter, both of whose legs were wounded by the same bullet that penetrated one of his legs. One of the hoped-for prizes was a Vickers machine gun that continued to fire until the sergeant and the four men who had been operating it died. One soldier managed to shoot Allman in the chest and he died soon afterwards. The only other volunteer who died was Jimmy Baily, who had been firing from the embankment.

The number of British fatalities remains obscure. The official statement after the event admitted to no more that one officer and six other ranks, with twelve wounded. These figures were challenged by local people, who claimed that twelve coffins or more were later removed from Killarney.

The shooting continued for about fifty minutes until word came that the Mallow train was nearing the station with an army officer on the footplate. Some of the volunteers opened fire immediately and were assailed by a fierce fusillade. McEllistrim, now in command after the death of Allman, signalled a retreat and those who could moved quickly south and headed for open country, mostly turf bog, swept by machine-gun fire as they ran. The rest crossed the River Flesk to safety. When they later met for debriefing they found that they had just eight rounds of ammunition left and had not managed to capture any of the enemy weapons.

Tourmakeady
3 May 1921

Tourmakeady is an Irish-speaking village on the western shore of Lough Mask in the heart of County Mayo. With the long range of the Partry Mountains behind and the great stretch of the lough running south it is a very picturesque location. It was here that Coláiste Chonnacht, the second of the summer colleges established by the Gaelic League, was opened in 1905. Sixteen years later it was the site of the first significant encounter between the IRA and the Crown forces in County Mayo during the Tan War.

The South Mayo Brigade of the IRA had prime intelligence that a two-vehicle party of the RIC was bringing stores from Bermingham's shop in Ballinrobe to the barracks at Derrypark, south of the village. Tom Maguire, the commander, chose a sharp bend on the main road as the site of an ambush. He assembled the Ballinrobe flying column and combined them with volunteers from local companies to make a striking force of sixty. These he divided into three companies, placing one at the southern end of the village under the command of Paddy May. He took charge of the second unit at the centre of the village, while Michael O'Brien led the final group to the Fair Green at the northern end. The villagers were placed under guard and advised to remain quiet and well away from the windows.

The two cars travelled, as was customary, about 300 yards apart, and the first was allowed to drive right through the village until it reached the spot where May's group were in hiding behind a wall opposite the gates of Drumbane House. May opened fire, killing the driver, Constable Christopher Patrick O'Regan, and causing the car to crash into the gates. The other occupants dismounted and began to return fire. By now the second vehicle had reached the Fair Green and had stopped when O'Brien's unit began to shoot. Seeing that his men were not in combat May sent one half to the Fair Green and the rest to Drumbane. With these reinforcements he soon overcame the remaining RIC men in the leading car, killing three constables: Herbert Oakes, William Power and John Regan. The occupants of the Crossley ran into a small local hotel and began firing. At this point Maguire gave orders to withdraw and seek shelter in the Partry mountains.

What happened next is a matter of serious historical confusion, to put it euphemistically. Both sides gave vastly different accounts of the aftermath. The IRA version is that a large force of British reinforcements attacked them in the mountains and things were looking very bad until the 1st (Castlebar) Battalion of the West Mayo Brigade under the command of Commandant Michael Kilroy came to their rescue. In the fighting that followed Michael O'Brien was killed and Tom Maguire wounded. So fierce was the fighting that the army withdrew from the Partries and shortly afterwards the isolated RIC barracks at Cuilmore, Derrypark and Kinnury were abandoned. Dublin Castle and GHQ issued statements claiming that they had managed to capture 'a large body of rebels' in Tourmakeady. At that stage of the war, when frightful deeds were perpetrated by both sides, the need for propaganda victories were paramount and truth was the main victim.

Modreeny, County Tipperary
3 June 1921

Modreeny is on the road about four miles from Borrisokane, more than half-way to Cloughjordan in County Tipperary. On 3 June 1921, a party of RIC men on bicycles was on its way to Cloughjordan where they had court duties. They were followed by a sixteen-man military patrol transported by three cars and a lorry. The expedition came to the attention of the North Tipperary flying column, under the command of Commandant Sean Gaynor and Commandant Jack Collinson (who took over from Gaynor for the period of the ambush). The joint military and RIC company amounted to forty-three men while the IRA total was seventeen. When the operation was first suggested the only known enemy force were the dozen mounted policemen; the presence of he army and their superior equipment, including a heavy machine gun mounted on the back of the army truck, came as something of a shock.

In spite of the disparity as regards men and weapons Gaynor decided to attack, choosing a double bend at the cross for the precise point of impact. The local unit was joined by five volunteers from Cloughjordan armed with shotguns, not the usual weapon for flying squads but lethal enough at close range.

When the shooting began Constable James Briggs, a decorated ex-soldier from Wigtown in Scotland, died instantly under the hail of bullets. His companions, Constable John Cantlon, a native of Carlow, Constable Martin Feeney from Roscommon and Constable William Walsh from Queen's County, died of their wounds the next day. The response capacity of the Crown forces was limited by the accidental decommissioning of the machine-gun when one of the IRA's shots hit it by chance. The lorry withdrew and after a further exchange of shots the flying columns disappeared. The farmer who was suspected of being an informer would surely have been shot had he not managed to conceal himself under some straw and escape in the confusion of the withdrawal. Later, in reprisal, six houses in the neighbourhood, the property of known republican sympathisers, were set on fire by Crown forces.

The War of Independence ended or at least hesitated with the Truce that was declared on 11 July 1921. During 1921, 235 policemen had died, with fifty-six casualties in the month of May alone, making it the most violent period in the whole of the Tan War. The campaign continued right until zero hour with two killings on the actual day; Sergeant James King was shot as he cycled from his home to the barracks in Castlerea, County Roscommon, and Constable Alexander Clarke was killed as he walked to his lodgings in Skibbereen, County Cork. These actions were rooted in the exaltation of the IRA, secure in their moral authority since the Dáil had stated in January 1919 that a state of war existed between Ireland and Great Britain. Not all Irish people however, were not comfortable with the killing of the ordinary members of the RIC, who were mostly Catholic and from rural Ireland.

THE CIVIL WAR 1922-3

DUBLIN
28 JUNE-5 JULY 1922

The first battle in the Civil War was fought in Dublin, six months after the acceptance (and non-acceptance by a minority) of the Treaty. There had been already some flickerings of anti-Treaty activity around the country that Richard Mulcahy (1886-1971), the Free State GOC, had tried to quench but the fact that most of the charismatic leaders from the 'Tan' War were now 'Irregular' meant that conflict was inevitable. The occupation of the Four Courts on 14 April 1922 by militants led by Rory O'Connor (1883-1922) was the beginning of the undeclared war. The assassination of Sir Henry Wilson (1864-1922) on 22 June, followed by strong pressure from the British, and the arrest of the Free State general J.J. 'Ginger' O'Connell by Irregulars on 27 June meant that Michael Collins (1890-1922) and Mulcahy had little option but to move against the Four Courts garrison.

General Macready (1862-1945), the British GOC, who had been ordered to attack the Four Courts, wisely ignored his instructions; he had worked too hard for peace to risk the collapse of the Treaty. He did, however, provide the artillery for the Free State army. Guns were set up just across the Liffey from the courts, on Parliament Street and Winetavern Street and bombardment began at 4am on 28 June. Among the members of the Republican executive inside were Rory O'Connor, Joe McKelvey, Liam Mellows (1892-1922) and Ernie O'Malley (1898-1957), the last acting as commander. The early volleys had little effect on the stout walls of the complex. Two more cannon were supplied by

Macready, along with the offer of howitzers and even an RAF bomber, which Collins rejected as likely to cause many civilian casualties. (In fact when the battle for Dublin came to an end on 5 July it was discovered that there had been more than 250 civilian deaths.) On 29 June the Free State army stormed and occupied the east wing of the Four Courts. By then most of the fabric was on fire and a desperate appeal for help from Republican forces outside resulted in a correspondingly downbeat response from Oscar Traynor (1886-1963), commander of the IRA in Dublin, urging them to surrender; he did not have the forces to help them and needed to organise resistance in Wicklow.

At 3.30pm on 30 June O'Malley surrendered what was left of the Four Courts to Brigadier General Paddy Daly. It was a costly venture, leaving one of Dublin's finest buildings a smouldering ruin– but already the country as a whole had suffered an even more grievous – and irreparable – injury. Some hours before the surrender there was a mighty explosion from the western block of the complex. It made the sound of the artillery fire seem trivial and fifty Free State soldiers were injured as a cloud of dark smoke blocked out the June afternoon sky. It was almost certainly caused by the flames reaching the Public Records Office, the area that the Irregulars had chosen as their arms and explosive store. Tossed amid the dense black and dusty clouds was a myriad small pieces of white parchment, vellum and paper as the documentary evidence of nearly a thousand years of Ireland's history was unmercifully shredded.

The battle of Dublin did not finish with the surrender of the Four Courts; there was an epilogue, what contemporary Dubliners would have called a 'tilly'. Traynor and his men had taken over the north-east side of Sackville Street, as Dublin's main thoroughfare was then known, concentrated in a group of buildings known as the 'Block'. They also commandeered four hotels, the Gresham, Crown, Granville and Hammam. Their move was meant primarily as a diversion to take some of the heat away from the Four Courts and they kept up steady fire in the iconic street that had seen the beginning of the revolution six years before when Pearse read the Proclamation of the Irish Republic on the steps of the GPO.

When the wreckage of the Four Courts was made secure the provisional government's forces were deployed against the 'Block' and the other Irregular positions. The only Irregular position on the west side of the street was the YMCA building but it was soon put out of action by an underground mine. Gradually Free State forces were able to surround the little pocket of resistance, with cannon at Henry Street, Gardiner Street, Parnell Street and Beresford Place, at the foot of lower Abbey Street. Most of the east side of Sackville Street was ablaze and Traynor gave orders for his men to try to slip out individually and make their way to Blessington, County Wicklow, the nearest Irregular stronghold.

A rearguard force of fifteen led by Cathal Brugha (1874-1922) stayed behind the Hammam, which was already burning. By the afternoon of 5 July it was clear that they could hold out no longer and Brugha ordered a surrender at 5pm. He stayed behind and then appeared at the door alone, brandishing a revolver. This was interpreted as a sign that he was not part of the general surrender and he was shot in the thigh by a Free State marksman. There was no suggestion that the shot had been intended to kill him but he died later of blood loss. The battle of Dublin was at last over. Forty-nine Irregulars had been killed and 158 wounded, while the figures for the Free State army were sixteen dead and 122 wounded.

LIMERICK
2-20 JULY 1922

By the end of the first week of June 1922 the steadily growing
Free State army was in control of Leinster after successfully
ousting Irregulars from Louth, Wicklow and Wexford. Already
the east-west split had been effected and the concept of the
'Munster Republic' was taking shape. Liam Lynch (1893-1923),
now Chief of Staff of the Anti-Treaty IRA, had decided that
maintaining a defensive position behind a line linking Limerick
and Waterford and involving such towns as Carrick-on-Suir,
Clonmel, Fethard and Cashel, would force a renegotiation of the
Treaty and effectively prevent the practical existence of the Free
State. Holding Limerick was essential to this strategy, which was
strongly disapproved of by younger Republicans like O'Malley
and Tom Barry (1897-1980). The Free State who had been active
guerrilla leaders knew that the Irregular forces were greatly in
the majority and had many effective military leaders. They were
also aware that recruitment in the Free State army was increasing
daily and that Collins and Mulcahy could be sure of strong
support from Britain, especially in supplying the artillery that the
Irregulars totally lacked.

Limerick was already, by a narrow margin, Irregulars in its
politics. It was one of the places outside Dublin where disaffection
had been noticed as early as February 1922. The Irregulars held
the four barracks with their headquarters in the newest one,
Sarsfield. They also held the two bridges over the Shannon. The
Provisional Government forces held the Customs House, the jail,

the courthouse, the RIC barracks in William Street and Cruise's Hotel. Most of these were central sites; they also controlled the Athlunkard Bridge over the Abbey River, the Shannon's tributary, a little to the north, which gave them access to the east.

From the beginning of July 1922 the two sides were sizing each other up, the Free State forces conscious of their lack of firepower. Their commander, Donnchadh O'Hannigan, made no serious move until reinforcements arrived on 11 July and began the battle for Limerick at 7pm that evening when he opened fire on the Ordnance Barracks.

Over the next eight days the centre of the city was the scene of bitter street-fighting around the axis of William Street, where the Free State forces had their headquarters in the former RIC barracks. When the fighting began, Lynch withdrew from Limerick and set up the Anti-Treaty headquarters in Clonmel, thirty-five miles to the south-east. During the fighting the balance of superiority swung like a pendulum: street positions were lost and won again as armoured cars were used to smash down barricades and retake salient positions like the Munster Tavern. Shops were shut and civilians were at great risk not only of crossfire but also of extreme hunger as food was unobtainable. Free State success was doubtful until the arrival on 17 July of General Eoin O'Duffy (1892-1944) with 150 men and armaments including 400 rifles, ten Lewis guns, 400 grenades and, crucially, an eighteen-pounder field gun.

The Free State GHQ was equally aware of the need to hold the city and made 18 July the day of a general attack on Republican positions. Even the new rifles and grenades used in the sudden sallies that had characterised most of the battle for Limerick had no measurable effect. And so with some reluctance on 19 July the Free State soldiers set up the field gun on Arthur's Quay and used it to batter down the four-foot-thick walls of the Strand Barracks.

The Civil War was always a war between old comrades and many attempts were made by both sides throughout its ten-months duration to avoid bloodshed and sue for truces. Just before the bombardment of the barracks a messenger was sent to tell the Irregulars that shelling would begin in five minutes and advise the garrison under Captain Connie McNamara to surrender. It was not a very generous offer but tension between the two sides had been growing during the previous week. Two nurses from the staff of the Red Cross hospital located beside the barracks came back with a message from McNamara that he would never surrender while he had ammunition. When the nurses had returned to their hospital the shelling commenced. The barracks were pounded all day until, by 8pm, there was a gap in the rear wall big enough for troops to enter. A group of twelve men led by Captain Con O'Halloran stormed through the breach, shooting and hurling grenades. They in turn were attacked from O'Connell Street. Immediately these Irregulars were subject to a machine-gun enfilade from the northern bank of the Shannon as they tried to cross William Street and Thomas Street which runs parallel to it.

O'Halloran's storming party met with strong opposition from inside the parade ground. O'Halloran himself was wounded in the chest by machine-gun bullets. By now the buildings of the barracks were blazing furiously but a majority of the garrison was using the confusion of the fire and the efforts of their rearguard to escape, mostly through the hospital next door. By midnight all the military barracks in the city were blazing, as were the other Irregular strongholds. Up to two thirds of the Irregulars managed to escape from Limerick after the fall of the city to the Provisional Government. They went south towards Bruree, mining the roads, felling trees and blowing up bridges, and set up a field of operations in the Bruree-Bruff-Kilmallock triangle, twenty miles from Limerick.

WATERFORD
18-21 JULY 1922

Like Limerick, Waterford was under the control of the Anti-Treaty forces from the beginning of July 1922. As the eastern boundary of the 'Munster Republic' it was regarded as important not only tactically but symbolically. Like Limerick the details of its topography were significant in the battle for control. The city is built mainly on the south bank of the River Suir, 250 yards wide at that point, and reached from the north by a cantilever bridge, called after Edmund Ignatius Rice (1762-1844), the founder of the Irish Christian Brothers. It was desirable that this bridge be available for any attacking force and one of the priorities for the forces of the provisional government was its maintenance. It was also a priority of Commandant 'Pax' Whelan who commanded the city garrison of Irregulars: he was there first and caused the bridge to be raised.

The Irregulars occupied significant buildings in the town: the post office, hotels, boarding-houses, military barracks, the eleventh-century Reginald's Tower by the riverside and Ballybricken Jail. They also took over city transport, the primitive telecommunications network and stores. The Free State troops were led by Major-General John T. Prout, who five years earlier had served with the American Expeditionary Force in France, and a local man, Brigadier Patrick Paul, who had also served in the World War I. They had brought with them 700 men, four armoured cars and eighteen-pounder cannon that they set up on Mercy Hill, known locally as 'Misery' Hill. For fear of causing too much damage to property and the loss of civilian lives they positioned the gun on the side away from the town but this proved ineffective. Paul ordered the cannon to be relocated to the summit where it attracted mainly ineffectual fire. He directed fire at the infantry barracks, the artillery barracks and the prison. (Paul had a moment of terror when one of the shells directed at the artillery barracks fell short and damaged his own house, injuring his mother.)

The bombardment was beginning to have the effect he intended. The Irregulars had no experience of shelling and, seeming to come from more than one gun, it unnerved them. They abandoned the positions but held grimly on to the post office and the various hotels where Whelan had billeted them.

The gun was then brought down to Ferrybank, further along the river, opposite the Mall, and fired 'open sights' until the Post Office too was set on fire and abandoned. That night a commando of a hundred Free State soldiers led by Captain Ned O'Brien crossed the Suir in a number of small boats and, taking the Irregulars by surprise, were able to dislodge them from positions along the quays. They took twelve prisoners and occupied the Adelphi and Imperial Hotels. One of the reasons for the stubborn resistance was the belief that a force of Irregulars was on its way from Carrick-on-Suir, eighteen miles to the west. This hope perished due to poor communications and the relief troops were ordered back to Carrick. Paul was left in charge of the ruinous city, ready to accept 500 rifles from the gunboat *Helga* to equip the surge of recruits to the National Army.

KILMALLOCK
21 JULY-5 AUGUST 1922

Kilmallock is a thriving market town twenty-one miles south of Limerick. It has a rich ecclesiastic and literary past and it was the centre of a series of intensive engagements during the Civil War. The nearby villages of Bruff, six miles to the north-east, and Bruree, four miles to the west, form a triangle with Kilmallock, and it was here that the Irregulars hoped for a convincing victory. Most of them were veterans of the 'Tan' war and they had retreated towards the triangle after they had abandoned Limerick. Their commander, Liam Deasy (1898-1974), was one of those later instrumental in finishing the war but, distressing as he found it, he continued to fight for a better treaty. The Irregulars had 2000 rifles and a few armoured cars, while the National Army had about 1400 rifles at the start of the campaign. Although largely inexperienced they had the advantage of having as second-in-command an experienced artillery officer, Major-General W.R.E. Murphy, who had served in the World War I as a Brigadier-General.

General Eoin O'Duffy (1892-1944) and Murphy began their campaign on Sunday 23 July by ousting Republican forces from Bruff. They made Kilmallock their next objective. They were twice beaten back and could not prevent their opponents from recapturing Bruff and taking seventy-six prisoners. O'Duffy decided upon a tactical retreat while he waited for reinforcements. His men retook Bruff but on the following Tuesday a unit of Free State troops was ambushed on a narrow road near the village and, although they fought their way through, suffered the loss of four men. On 30 July Murphy launched a determined attack on Bruree, using armoured cars and the mobile eighteen-pounder. The Republicans resisted fiercely for five hours until the artillery was brought into play and they too found it judicious to leave the scene. In one of those occasions when farce obtrudes into drama, the retreat was aided by a herd of cows that wandered in front of Murphy's artillery. Their presence was almost certainly not accidental; Bruree was Eamon de Valera's home place and the choice of the Kilmallock triangle by the Republicans was deliberate.

Deasy determined to recapture the town as it was essential to the defence of Kilmallock. On 2 August he sent a force of his men on a daring flanking move to take control of a village called Patrickswell, seven miles south of Limerick and well behind the Free State lines. The Republican commando had trench mortars and armoured cars. They were met with greater firepower and surrendered after being attacked by a second armoured car.

All attention was then focused on the defence of Kilmallock. The Free State troops had the advantage of continual reinforcements and increasing firepower but both Murphy and O'Duffy realised that the battle for Kilmallock could be a savage one. By 3 August the numbers in the Free State army in County Limerick had been increased to 4000 and Free State troops were able to surround the town completely. The Free State artillery began shelling two hills close to the town and were soon in control of them. When they entered the town they found it empty of Irregulars except for a rearguard of troops from Cork; the Republicans had once again slipped away. As it turned out there was no battle of Kilmallock.

DUNDALK
27 JULY-14 AUGUST 1922

With the Civil War now established some IRA commanders were placed in an awkward situation. This was especially true of Commandant Frank Aiken (1898-1983) commander of the 4th Northern Division of the IRA. His rejection of the Treaty was reluctant and his greater concern was the situation of Northern Catholics. They were in real danger from the UVF, now given an aura of respectability Ulster Special Constabulary, especially that section that would for nearly fifty years be known in infamy to the nationalist population in Ulster the B-Specials. Such concerns meant little to the Free State army who occupied Dundalk and imprisoned Aiken and his men in the military barracks. Two of Aiken's men, Campbell and Quigley, were shot while trying to escape. The army also released a number of 'B' Specials who were being held there by the IRA, enabling them to return to the North and continue their terror.

This gratuitous misreading of the situation in border areas enraged the usually phlegmatic Aiken and shook badly the neutral attitude he had hoped to maintain towards the new war. On 27 July, in an action reminiscent of the glory days of the recent 'Tan' War, the Irregular prisoners arranged for a mine to be exploded outside the barracks wall, allowing the Republican prisoners to escape through the breach. The device had been placed after the infiltration of Dundalk by 200 of Aiken's men from the 4th Northern Division. The resulting explosion shattered every window in the neighbourhood of the jail. In the general confusion

100 prisoners escaped, aided by the setting-up of barricades on the chief streets. At Quay Street an old Great Northern Railway locomotive was dragged from the marshalling yard to make pursuit difficult.

Early on the morning of 14 August, Aiken and his men reclaimed the barracks using mines and machine-gun fire. The devices were placed at the gate to Point Road, in the hospital, the officers' quarters, the HQ office block, the orderly office and guard room and went off with huge explosions. Other government implacements surrendered after minimal attack, netting the Republicans a useful haul of rifles, machine-guns and ammunition. A field gun was captured but, proving too difficult to transport, was spiked. Dundalk was now firmly in the hands of the Irregulars, to the considerable embarrassment of the Free State forces who had been so successful in dislodging Republican nests in other towns.

Three days later a government detachment under Commandant-General Dan Hogan and Colonel Hugo MacNeill attacked the Republicans in Dundalk. They concentrated on the barracks. For the first time in an Irish battle an aeroplane of the Royal Air Force was used to bomb the Republican defenders. Outgunned but still retaining the ammunition collected earlier from the town's military depots, Aiken decided on a judicious retreat, melting into the wild country of the Cooley peninsula and South Armagh, Aiken's home territory, where he and his column were safe both from Free State forces and B-Specials.

Cork
26 July-12 August 1922

By the last week of July 1922, Cork city was controlled by Republican forces, who occupied all the military and police barracks. Yet with the insistence on normality that ordinary people demonstrate under, the most abnormal circumstances the famous annual regatta was held as usual on 26 July. The city's position as the capital of the 'Munster Republic', to use the ambitious description of the absolutist leader Liam Lynch, had now less significance, as the other cities, Waterford and Limerick, fell to the Free State troops. There were, of course, many Irregulars in the city but not all agreed with the policies of the leadership, being concerned more with the condition of the oldest mercantile Irish city outside of Belfast. As July became August it was clear that the city was suffering not only from economic stagnation but from real want, with water rationing introduced and food supplies running dangerously low. It would probably have been an appropriate time to consider peace moves but as the situation of the Irregulars worsened Lynch became more resolutely determined to continue the war.

It was clear even to the diehards that Cork would become an object of attention to the Free State forces but attack was expected from the north and east as the army units from Limerick and Waterford inexorably occupied the smaller Munster towns. The Irregulars in the second city had to contend with opposition from its extensive bourgeoisie, the long-established, part-Protestant, merchant and professional classes. An attempt to impose a levy on the city merchants was met with mute resistance and the Republicans realised that the qualities needed for urban fiscal control were subtly different from those used to establish military supremacy. The invasion of Cork when it came was, to no one's surprise but that of the eager defenders, by sea. The forts guarding the Treaty ports were and would remain in British hands and it was a simple matter for the *Avronia* and the *Lady Wicklow*, Free State vessels, that had sailed from the North Wall in Dublin with more than 600 troops on Monday 7 August, to land near Cobh and move purposefully towards the city.

The Free State troops were led by General Emmet Dalton, with General Tom Ennis as second-in-command. They were helped by Commander H.C. Somerville, head of the Royal Navy in Cork, who provided them with a chart allowing the *Avronia* to make a safe path to Passage West, avoiding the mines the Irregulars had laid. The *Lady Wicklow* landed her contingent at Youghal, twenty miles east of the city and at Union hall in Glandore Harbour, approximately the same distance to the west. Opposition forces set off some of the mines to prevent the *Avronia* landing but they had no success. The village of Passage was taken after an hour's fighting and there was continual firing across the harbour for some time, until the British Admiralty banned ordinary shipping from attempting to use Cork Harbour.

When word came of the Free State landings a unit of the Irregulars was rushed to Rochestown. On their way they blew up the Cork-Crosshaven railway bridge to prevent the Free State forces travelling conveniently into the city centre. The terrain of steep hills and woods were to the advantage of the Anti-Treaty troops. Even when the Free State units attempted to advance from Passage they were unable to make any progress. The battle lasted for most of Wednesday, 9 August, the two forces engaged in a mile-wide sector between Ballincummins Cross and Doctor's Cross. There was much fighting, some of it hand-to-hand. Casualties were heavy but the stronger, better-armed, Free-State troops were clearly the imminent victors.

Cork had already suffered grievously during the War of Independence; the city centre had been fired by Black and Tans and Auxiliary forces on 11 December 1920. None of the citizens, except perhaps the most extreme of the Irregulars, relished the prospect of the city becoming a battlefield. The Irregulars decided to spare the city and finally evacuated it on Thursday, 10 August, having set fire to all the military installations. Before the holocaust their headquarters, the barracks on Union Quay, was stripped as if by a plague of white ants, with everything movable transferred to the convoy of lorries and cars assembled for retreat. Considerable looting took place before the final withdrawal. The whole force of Irregulars moved westwards, as many as could manage it on vehicles, the rest on bicycles or on foot. The old Muskerry railway was taken over, as were any trams capable of moving towards the west. Their progress was marked by a spotter plane.

When the Free State troops arrived they were welcomed by a majority of the populace. A proclamation issued on Saturday, 12 August, by government forces and signed by Emmet Dalton made it clear that they were in control but had no desire to interfere 'with the normal civilian activities of the community'. It made it clear that 'all arms, munitions, equipment and uniforms' were immediately to be 'delivered to the military authorities'. All items of stolen property were to be handed in to the police. The war was essentially over but the 'diehards', as many now called them, were only too determined to live up to the sobriquet. The war staggered bloodily on until he following May when on Liam Lynch's death, Aiken ordered the dumping of arms and a ceasefire.

THE BOGSIDE
12-14 AUGUST 1969

The battle of the Bogside in Derry represented the climax of the civil rights movement in Ulster and effectively the beginnings of the Northern Ireland 'Troubles' as they were euphemistically called. The clashes began about 2.30 in the afternoon of 12 August during the annual march of the Apprentice Boys to celebrate the lifting of the siege – the 'Relief of Derry' – 280 years earlier. (See Pages113–115) The Bogside is a nationalist area lying to the west of the city walls and close to the commercial centre. Since the RUC's (Royal Ulster Constabulary) attack on the civil rights march on 5 October the previous year tension in the city had been growing. A violent irruption by the RUC on 5 January had led to riots and the concept of 'Free Derry' that was painted on a gable wall presaged the 'no-go' area that the Bogside was to become.

Crash barriers set up to separate the Apprentice Boys marchers and their supporters from nationalist protesters became rallying points for both sides and when coins were thrown at the Apprentice Boys trouble was inevitable. A hail of missiles greeted even the nationalist community leaders, John Hume, Eddie McAteer and Ivan Cooper, who had been pleading for dispersal; Cooper was hit on the head. The first petrol bomb was thrown at 4.40pm, by which time the Apprentice Boys had begun to leave the city and the serious rioting started. A loyalist mob from the Waterside took part, fronted by and protected by the RUC. Even they, already damned as a sectarian force, were alarmed at the intensity of the violence and, protected by riot shields, tried to advance along Rossville Street, firing the missiles back at the largely young crowd. The eleven-storey block of Rossville flats that towered over the street gave the rioters a decided edge and the RUC were at a corresponding disadvantage. They made no attempt, however, to prevent the damage to property carried out by the crowd of loyalists well behind them.

From 11.00pm, William Street, Rossville Street and the street actually known as the Bogside filled up with CS gas. A volunteer group of paramedics, the Knights of Malta, attended to those suffering the effects of gas and others hurt by missiles and mismanaged petrol bombs. Old gasmasks issued during the Second World War were rooted out of cupboards and participants claimed that handkerchiefs soaked in vinegar acted quite well as filters. They gave no protection to the eyes, however, and since the night and the following day were heavy and calm without a breath of wind the gas was not easily dispersed. The police began to use live rounds and two men behind the barricade in Rossville Street were injured. Local doctors and nurses organised emergency hospitals. During the night several buildings were set on fire, with Stevenson's bakery and Richards's shirt factory gutted. Among the significant figures on the nationalist side was Bernadette Devlin a member of the People's Democracy who had been injured in a previous protest march at Burntollet Bridge and who acted as a kind of Joan of Arc. She tirelessly reviewed the Bogside defences, addressing the crowd through a loud-hailer.

By Thursday the battle assumed a kind of almost comic pattern: attacks from the nationalist side seemed to stop for meals. There was little or no action at lunch and teatime but the fighting was renewed with greater intensity after these lulls. By now Catholics of all classes felt the need to involve themselves in the struggle. There was a sense of the significance of what was already known as 'the Battle of the Bogside'. Television cameramen from international networks were recording each detail of the struggle. It was believed that one of the reasons for the lull at 6pm was the hope by the younger participants that they might see themselves on the 'telly'. The Irish government kept a close eye on the proceedings, calling an emergency cabinet meeting, and on the Wednesday evening Jack Lynch, the Fianna Fáil Taoiseach, stated on television: 'The government of Ireland can no longer stand by and see innocent people injured and perhaps worse.' In the cabinet strongest pressure came from Republican hardliners like Neil Blaney, who urged some unspecific invasion of Derry. Lynch, conscious of the effect such a move might have on the welfare of Catholics in Belfast, held firm but asked the British government to apply to the United Nations to send a peacekeeping force.

The terror in all nationalist minds was that the entirely sectarian and armed B-Specials, mobilised that evening, would swamp the Bogside and be happy to use live rounds. Lynch did order units of the Irish army stationed near Letterkenny to set up properly equipped field hospitals at the border, at most five miles from the scene of the fighting. Stronger lobbying of James Callaghan, the Home Secretary by John Hume and others finally persuaded him to authorise the deployment of the British army. They appeared on the streets at 6.00 some from the local Ebrington barracks but mostly from the troopship *Sir Tristram*. They assembled in Guildhall Square and Shipquay Street before moving to Waterloo Place and William Street. As they arrived the exhausted RUC moved gratefully out. The Battle of the Bogside was over.

Afterword

It is hard to recall now the surge of euphoria that the nationalist population in Derry experienced after the Battle of the Bogside. The British soldiers were fêted and courted in a way that was reminiscent of newsreel footage of the Allied armies as they liberated towns in occupied Europe at the end of the Second World War. Two days later they were sent into the streets of Belfast after many nationalists were burnt out of their houses in UVF rioting that also resulted in eleven Catholic casualties. The general in charge, Sir Ian Freeland, warned that the honeymoon was not likely to last: events over nearly forty years proved his words only too accurate. The 'Troubles' as they were euphemistically called led to thousands dead, lots more injured and the destruction of many buildings.

Westminster learned slowly from the lessons of all the dark events such as Bloody Sunday, Bloody Friday, the UWC strike and the IRA hunger strike. The persistence of the British government, with strong support from the Irish government, eventually led to the Good Friday Agreement of 1998 and an agreed legislative assembly that is now dominated by reluctant bedfellows, the Democratic Unionist Party and Sinn Féin. Life in the assembly has its difficulties and the threat of dual sovereignty by Westminster and Dublin is always present but the people of Northern Ireland are war-weary and apart from dissident republican bands most of the combatants on both sides have put their weapons beyond use. Perhaps the little boy who asked his teacher, 'What are the Troubles?' was the true voice of the future.

In time, too, the suspicion and fear that the two warring tribes have felt intermittently since the original seventeenth-century plantation, may lessen and sectarianism cease to be the chief characteristic of warring Ulster. After all the battles fought between the two countries on Irish soil, relations between the Republic and the UK, improved by the years of negotiation that culminated in the Good Friday Agreement, are more cordial than ever before.

Selected Bibliography

Abbott, R. *Police Casualties in Ireland 1919–1922*. Cork, 2000.

Bardon, J. *A History of Ireland in 250 Episodes*. Dublin, 2008.

Barry, T. Guerrilla Days in Ireland. Dublin 1949.

Bartlett, T. & Jeffrey, K. (eds.) *A Military History of Ireland*. Cambridge, 1996.

Bell, J. Bowyer. *The Secret Army: A History of the IRA*. Dublin. 1970.

Bredin, (Brig.) A.C.E. *A History of the Irish Soldier*. Belfast, 1987.

Ellis, Peter Berresford. *The Boyne Water*. London, 1976.

Caulfield, M. *The Easter Rebellion*. Dublin, 1995.

Clarke, A. *The Old English in Ireland*. London, 1966.

Deasy, L. *Brother against Brother*. Cork, 1982.

Doherty, J.E. & Hickey, D.J. *A Chronology of Irish History since 1500*. Dublin, 1989.

——————. *A New Dictionary of Irish History from 1800*. Dublin, 2003

Doherty, R. *The Siege of Derry*. Stroud, 2008.

Dwyer, T.R. *Tans, Terror and Troubles: Kerry's Real Fighting Story*. Cork, 2001.

Foster, R.F. *Modern Ireland 1600–1972*. London, 1988.

Hart, Peter. *The IRA and Its Enemies*. Oxford, 1998.

Hayes-McCoy, G.H.. London, 1969.

Kee, Robert. London, 1971.

Lyons, F.S.L. *Ireland Since the Famine*. London, 1971.

McCann, E. *War and an Irish Town*. London, 1974.

Mulcahy, R. *My Father, the General: Richard Mulcahy and the Military History of the Revolution*. Dublin, 2009.

Murtagh, H. *The Battle of the Boyne*. Drogheda, 2006.

Neeson, Eoin. *The Civil War. 1922–1923*. Dublin, 1989.

Ó Conchubair, B. (ed.) *Kerry's Fighting Story 1916–21*. Cork, 2009.

——————. (ed.) *Limerick's Fighting Story 1916–21*. Cork, 2009.

Ó Corráin. Donncha. *Ireland before the Normans.* Dublin, 1972.

O'Faolain, S. The Great O'Neill. London,1942.

Ó Siochrú, M. *God's Executioner: Oliver Cromwell and the Conquest of Ireland.* London, 2008.

Pakenham, T. *The Year of Liberty.* London, 1969.

Póirtéir, Cathal. (ed.) *The Great Irish Rebellion of 1798.* Cork, 1998.

Roche. R. *The Norman Invasion of Ireland.* Dublin, 1970.

Simms, J.G. *The Siege of Derry.* Dublin, 1966.

Stewart, A.T.Q. *The Summer Soldiers: The 1798 Rebellion in Antrim and Down.* Belfast, 1995.

Index of Battles